Economies of Gender

The Politics of Marriage and Gender:
Global Issues in Local Contexts

Series Editor: Péter Berta

The Politics of Marriage and Gender: Global Issues in Local Context series from Rutgers University Press fills a gap in research by examining the politics of marriage and related practices, ideologies, and interpretations, and addresses the key question of how the politics of marriage has affected social, cultural, and political processes, relations, and boundaries. The series looks at the complex relationships between the politics of marriage and gender, ethnic, national, religious, racial, and class identities, and analyzes how these relationships contribute to the development and management of social and political differences, inequalities, and conflicts.

For a complete list of titles in the series, please see the last page of the book.

Economies of Gender

Masculinity, "Mail Order Brides," and Women's Labor

JULIA H. MESZAROS

RUTGERS UNIVERSITY PRESS

NEW BRUNSWICK, CAMDEN, AND NEWARK, NEW JERSEY

LONDON AND OXFORD

Rutgers University Press is a department of Rutgers, The State University of New Jersey, one of the leading public research universities in the nation. By publishing worldwide, it furthers the University's mission of dedication to excellence in teaching, scholarship, research, and clinical care.

Names: Meszaros, Julia H., author.
Title: Economies of gender: masculinity, "mail order brides,"
and women's labor / Julia H. Meszaros.
Description: New Brunswick, New Jersey : Rutgers University Press, [2025] |
Series: Politics of marriage and gender: global issues in local contexts |
Includes bibliographical references and index.
Identifiers: LCCN 2024060372 (print) | LCCN 2024060373 (ebook) |
ISBN 9781978842779 (paperback ; alk. paper) |
ISBN 9781978842786 (hardback; alk. paper) | ISBN 9781978842793 (epub)
Subjects: LCSH: Dating (Social customs) | Man-woman relationships. |
Human trafficking. | Foreign spouses.
Classification: LCC HQ801 .M543 2025 (print) | LCC HQ801 (ebook) |
DDC 306.82—dc23/eng/20250221
LC record available at https://lccn.loc.gov/2024060372
LC ebook record available at https://lccn.loc.gov/2024060373

A British Cataloging-in-Publication record for this book is available
from the British Library.

References to internet websites (URLs) were accurate at the time of writing. Neither the author nor Rutgers University Press is responsible for URLs that may have expired or changed since the manuscript was prepared.

∞ The paper used in this publication meets the requirements of the American National Standard for Information Sciences—Permanence of Paper for Printed Library Materials, ANSI Z39.48-1992.

rutgersuniversitypress.org

For Csilla and Attila Meszaros

CONTENTS

SERIES FOREWORD

The politics of marriage (and divorce) is an often-used strategic tool in various social, cultural, economic, and political identity projects as well as in symbolic conflicts between ethnic, national, or religious communities. Despite having multiple strategic applicabilities, pervasiveness in everyday life, and huge significance in performing and managing identities, the politics of marriage is surprisingly underrepresented both in the international book publishing market and the social sciences.

The Politics of Marriage and Gender: Global Issues in Local Contexts is a series from Rutgers University Press examining the politics of marriage as a phenomenon embedded into and intensely interacting with much broader social, cultural, economic, and political processes and practices such as globalization; transnationalization; international migration; human trafficking; vertical social mobility; the creation of symbolic boundaries between ethnic populations, nations, religious denominations, or classes; family formation; or struggles for women's and children's rights. The series primarily aims to analyze practices, ideologies, and interpretations related to the politics of marriage, and to outline the dynamics and diversity of relatedness—interplay and interdependence, for instance—between the politics of marriage and the broader processes and practices mentioned above. In other words, most books in the series devote special attention to how the politics of marriage and these processes and practices mutually shape and explain each other.

The series concentrates on, among other things, the complex relationships between the politics of marriage and gender, ethnic, national, religious, racial, and class identities globally, and examines how these relationships contribute to the development and management of social, cultural, and political differences, inequalities, and conflicts.

The series seeks to publish single-authored books and edited volumes that develop a gap-filling and thought-provoking critical perspective, that are well-balanced between a high degree of theoretical sophistication and empirical richness, and that cross or rethink disciplinary, methodological, or theoretical boundaries. The thematic scope of the series is intentionally left broad to encourage creative submissions that fit within the perspectives outlined above. Among the potential topics closely connected with the problem sensitivity of the series are "honor"-based violence; arranged (forced, child, etc.) marriage; transnational marriage markets, migration, and brokerage; intersections of marriage and religion/class/race; the politics of agency and power within marriage; reconfiguration of family: same-sex marriage/union; the politics of love, intimacy, and desire; marriage and multicultural families; the (religious, legal, etc.) politics of divorce; the causes, forms, and consequences of polygamy in contemporary societies; sport marriage; refusing marriage; and so forth.

Economies of Gender: Masculinity, "Mail Order Brides," and Women's Labor is a fascinating account of how the international dating industry works and why it is especially popular among male participants. Based on transnational participant observation carried out in the former Soviet Union, Latin America, and Southeast Asia, Julia H. Meszaros convincingly argues that when we perform genders in the contexts of international dating, we also deal with "various forms of labor that create gendered forms of capital and value." The monograph pays special attention to the continuously changing content and dynamics of "femininity capital" that derives from various forms of women's labor that are associated with femininity (aesthetic, emotional, intimate, reproductive, and sexual). The author also explores how and why "femininity capital" is exploited by men and society—embedding the contemporary analysis of the concept into wider perspectives such as gender history, the politics of hierarchies of geographic locations, or the racialized international division of reproductive labor. *Economies of Gender: Masculinity, "Mail Order Brides," and Women's Labor* is a thought-provoking attempt to understand in a more nuanced way the subtle interplays between gender ideologies and practices, labor and other markets, capitals, value regimes, and identities.

Péter Berta
University College London,
School of Slavonic and
East European Studies /
Budapest Business School,
Department of Communication

Economies of Gender

Introduction

Masculinity as Access to Women's Labor

The concept of the "mail order bride" and international dating has shifted in recent years with the popularity of the television show *90 Day Fiancé* and the growing phenomenon of passport bros on TikTok and other social media platforms. For the past fifty years, the term "mail order bride" has been used pejoratively, as the term seems to imply that women abroad can be purchased and trafficked across borders. Numerous scholars in anthropology and gender studies have conducted interviews and studies of women who participate in the international dating industry, challenging the common misperception of mail order brides as victims of human trafficking and demonstrating these women's motivations for finding husbands from Western countries. Since there are numerous studies documenting the agency of women participants in international dating, this book focuses on the experiences and motivations of the male participants and the workings of the industry in general.

90 Day Fiancé began in 2014, highlighting the relationships of U.S. citizens with their foreign partners who go through the K-1 fiancé visa process and must get married within ninety days. The popularity of the show and the commentary surrounding the participants in online spaces like Reddit and TikTok highlight a few common narratives that characterize cross-border relationships between people in the "West" and those from outside of it: (1) The non-Western partner is only looking for money or a way to gain legal entry into the United States, or (2) the Western partner is someone who cannot find a decent and willing partner in their home dating market because they are defective in some way (socially awkward, unattractive, violent, etc.).[1]

The story of David and Lana on the fourth season of *90 Day Fiancé: Before the 90 Days*, one of the many TLC spinoffs from the *90 Day* franchise, exemplifies the stereotypes associated with the mail order bride industry and the websites that facilitate these relationships. In David's storyline, he can only contact

Lana through the messaging feature on the dating website he met her on, which is a reality of what I call the international dating industry. Due to legal regulations in the international dating industry by the International Marriage Broker Regulation Act (IMBRA), all communication between couples must happen through the dating agency's website until the couple has met in person. The season followed David on his fifth attempt to meet Lana in person after she did not meet him on his first four trips to Ukraine. Viewers on Reddit and other social media venues tended to characterize his relationship as a "scam" for money. Eventually, Lana shows up in real life but has no real interest in cultivating a serious relationship with David.

The producers of the show obviously choose the most mismatched couples in terms of age differences, families, and attractiveness in order to create more dramatic television. A large percentage of the couples on the show met through some sort of website, but David is one of the few stories following a man who utilized a true international dating website. The mainstreaming of cross-cultural relationships through shows like *90 Day* has had an interesting impact on the international dating industry in recent years, helping to normalize international dating in general. The phenomenon has expanded toward increasing numbers of Black men, who are calling themselves "passport bros" and heading to Colombia or the Philippines in search of a more traditional woman. Within the twelve years I spent following the industry, it has moved from a fringe phenomenon associated with older white men toward being more normalized for men of all ages and races.

Years after I finished my fieldwork in the international dating industry, I arrived in Los Angeles to attend the annual American Sociological Association meeting in August 2022. After years of chatting, I decided to invite one of my research participants, Nikola, out for dinner.[2] Nikola and I have been chatting for years about his participation in international dating through formalized, for-profit international dating agencies. Unlike most of the men I met throughout my time following the industry, Nikola is in his early thirties and from a conservative Mexican family based in Los Angeles. Despite strong cultural ties to Mexico, Nikola often would disassociate from a Latino identity. After months of chatting about his background and life, he revealed to me that he had legally changed his name to something less obviously Latino than his given name. He told me, "I immediately got more job offers when I changed my name on my resume."[3] Nikola works in the IT industry but also does many side jobs, such as fixing people's computers for cash, in an attempt to earn as much money as possible to fulfill his dream of moving abroad to Ukraine or Russia.

Nikola arrived to pick me up from my hotel in an Uber, dressed up to go out to dinner and a comedy show. We had not spoken since the Russian invasion of Ukraine in February and I was curious to see how Nikola interpreted this news for his future plans to move to one of those two countries. As we discussed the unfolding invasion of Ukraine, Nikola began explaining to me that he had been trying to help individual women in Ukraine by sending them money. He continually wanted to invest in learning Russian and talked about wanting to move to Ukraine in order to help rebuild the country as an entrepreneur. In a previous interview many years before, Nikola mentioned that an older man mentioned to him that the best time to find a wife who could be a model is during the breakdown of society; that when women are more economically desperate, he would find the type of model he was looking to marry. With the ongoing economic and political instability characterizing Ukrainian life since the Russian invasion in February of 2022, Nikola felt like he would finally be able to access the Ukrainian woman of his dreams.

Unlike many of the older men I met on romance tours, Nikola utilized the language and ideology of contemporary misogyny lifted from social movements associated with the online manosphere, such as Involuntary Celibates, Pick Up Artists and Men Going Their Own Way (MGTOW).[4] While each of these groups has different particular beliefs, they utilize similar language and accept the "red pill" philosophy, a reference to the film *The Matrix*. By accepting the red pill philosophy, men are "awakened" to the realities of feminist overreach in the West that allow women to dominate the sexual marketplace and society in general, thus upsetting the "natural" order of gender and evolutionary biology. Men who adopt red pill philosophies argue that men's positions are declining in Western societies, creating a number of social problems. Each community in the manosphere has a different solution for dealing with society's misandry. For example, the mass shooter Elliot Rodger in Santa Barbara and mass van attacker Alek Minassian in Toronto were both inspired by their involvement in online incel communities.

Canadian psychology professor and self-help author Jordan Peterson defends gender roles as a part of an ahistorical unchanging binary based on reproduction and gained notoriety within various manosphere communities for refusing to use transgender people's preferred gender pronouns. Popular social media influencer and mixed martial arts (MMA) fighter Andrew Tate goes further by normalizing the sexual exploitation of women online for monetary gain, which he is currently (2024) being investigated for in Romania. Men within the manosphere complain about the deregulation of women's sexuality and increasing financial independence, which they believe provides women with the power of choice in the sexual market, leaving men vulnerable and alone. Nikola told me about a blonde, white woman he was obsessed with during his early twenties, and how she was this hot, rich stereotypical Los Angeles woman who brushed him off for his lack of money and ethnicity. This rejection shaped his interest in red pill communities and the international dating industry.

Nikola explained to me that at first he considered himself an incel, angry at all "hot" women that seemed out of his reach, but he later shifted toward

MGTOW principles by refusing to date any more Western women.[5] However, Nikola counters some important MGTOW principles by still wanting to marry a woman from Ukraine or Russia, as MGTOW encourages men to abandon marrying women altogether. During his time on a romance tour with the company Dream Connections in Ukraine, Nikola encountered a group of four other men with similar political views about gender and heterosexual relationships: "We [he and his tour mates] thought similar, like, feminism has raised up a very toxic culture. And it's been very toxic that straight men are now in a sense losing their position in society . . . as a man, you can't even behave like a man. You are immediately judged; you are immediately humiliated as a characterless person." He and the four other men he met on tour developed a strong bond and still chat with each other to this day, as Nikola explained to me that conservative men like himself do not really fit in with the vibe of Southern California.

Ultimately, Nikola and his friends traced their dissatisfaction with dating in Western societies to the increasing expectations of equality within heterosexual relationships fostered by feminism. As Nikola explained to me, he felt that in Ukraine, unlike in the United States, he could still be "the man" in his relationships with women: "Coming back from Ukraine, I realized how feminism is growing so fast and changing everything, feminism is making everything so toxic. So, I came back and had an argument with a friend that back in Ukraine everything is easy, it's not a problem, you should be a gentleman, you can be a man, you can buy girls flowers." For Nikola and his friends, feminism is equated with women acting "masculine"; not wanting flowers, not doing their hair/makeup, not wearing feminine clothing (such as high heels), and embracing body size positivity for overweight women. Many of the things Nikola and his friends associated with femininity, as well as society at large, are based around a certain definition of womanhood that relies on women's invisiblized labor: wearing certain clothing and participating in certain grooming practices, such as makeup, exercise, dieting, hair removal, and hair styling.

Throughout my twelve years following the international dating industry, men continually shared stories of disappointment, loneliness, and frustration with their previous relationships in Western countries. As I have discussed in prior publications, men told me that they lack access to women's labor in the West and that femininity is a scarce and valuable resource.[6] The majority of men began their descriptions of Western women in terms of their looks and claimed women simply no longer cared about maintaining themselves. The men I interviewed assumed that maintenance of one's physical appearance is a type of aesthetic labor that underlies femininity; men expect women to engage in this maintenance but often did not hold themselves to the same standards (one exception to this was Nikola, who consciously focused on dressing to impress).

The men I interviewed desired what they defined as "feminine": thin women who wore makeup, dressed in feminine clothing, and wore high heels. They complained that women in Western countries, particularly in the United States, did not perform the aesthetic labor they associated with femininity, such as having fat bodies, wearing casual clothing, and not wearing makeup. However, a significant number of the men over fifty years old that I met on romance tours did not maintain their physical appearance or hygiene in the same ways they expected women to. For most of the men I met, the youth and beauty available to them in other parts of the non-Western world were the main reason they joined the international dating industry.

Beyond desiring women's aesthetic and reproductive labors of femininity, men also desire intimate and sexual labor from their potential partners, which they also believe is unavailable to them in the West. The men I interviewed considered the sexual labor of women they were sexually attracted to in the West unattainable, as so few women performed the labor of remaining thin and aesthetically pleasing and the competition among men for access to thin, hot women is fierce. As Beth Montemurro demonstrates in her study of heterosexual men's understanding of their sexuality and masculinity, men sort themselves into hierarchies of masculinity based on the attractiveness of the women whose various forms of labor they can actually access.[7]

Nikola would continually tell me that his main goal was to find a "hot" wife who performed the appropriate aesthetic labors of femininity, and that he was not as worried about finding a wife interested in performing the reproductive labors of the home: "Today with technology we can just buy a robot vacuum, dishwasher, eat out. I don't need a woman to cook and clean. But these older tradcon guys prefer a woman who will cook and clean and take care of the house."[8] To Nikola, having a beautiful woman by his side as a type of "trophy wife" was more important than having a domestic maid in terms of moving higher in the hierarchy of men.

Thus, many of the men I spoke to throughout my time following the industry envision their relationships as a form of exchange, as they are often exchanging money for access to younger and more attractive women. The increase in demand for paid intimate services blurs the lines between the artificially separated spheres of intimate encounters and economic transactions. According to the sociologist Viviana Zelizer, in the traditional understanding of monetary transactions and intimacy, a sharp and hostile divide exists between the spheres of intimate relations and market transactions.[9] Therefore, people engage in important relational work within their relationships, determining what modes of payment are appropriate for each intimate relationship they cultivate, setting different expectations for different relationships. These "differentiated ties" that people develop in their intimate relationships demonstrate the complex negotiations that individuals are constantly making between the realm of the intimate and the economic. Thus, markets of commodified intimate labor are an important component of understanding the economies of gender that exist within heterosexual relationships.

Gender as Labor

In this book, I define heteromasculinity as the extraction of women's various forms of labor that are associated with femininity: aesthetic, reproductive, intimate, emotional, and sexual. These forms of labor have been defined by sociologists in terms of labor markets, both formal and informal. I aim to extend these definitions beyond the labor market to explore how they shape our understanding of gender within heterosexual relationships.

Sociologists Candace West and Don Zimmerman established the concept of "doing gender," which describes how individuals perform and present their gender in everyday life, influenced by social expectations and norms.[10] Feminist theorist Judith Butler argued that gender is not a fixed or stable identity, but rather a series of performances that are constantly being negotiated and performed in different social contexts.[11] When we "do gender," we are not only performing gender, but we are also engaging in various forms of labor that create gendered forms of capital and value.

The forms of labor associated with heteronormative femininity—such as aesthetic and reproductive labor—create what I refer to as "femininity capital." Men extract this femininity capital from women in order to create their own heteromasculinity capital. What I call "gendered capital" has been discussed as "erotic capital" or "sexual capital," highlighting the importance of beauty and sexuality in creating forms of capital, particularly for women.[12] The labor required to maintain femininity becomes a form of capital for women that Catherine Hakim argues can be utilized to get ahead in a society dominated by men's desires.[13]

Femininity capital holds significant value within heteronormative intimate relationships, as most heterosexual men determine their masculine capital and social value based on the type of women's labor they can access and extract. Women who generate substantial femininity capital through their labor—particularly aesthetic labor—enhance their value in the dating market. Men's masculinity capital and their position within the male hierarchy depend on their ability to extract the femininity capital of the most attractive women they can access. Thus, the expression of gender functions as an economy where bodies that possess the desired traits of femininity and conform to the "male gaze" are more highly valued in society. These women's bodies, often seen as "trophy wives," provide men with increased social capital and value.

Creating Femininity Capital

Catherine Hakim's concept of erotic capital builds on economic, social, and cultural forms of capital, and refers to the social appeal and physical attractiveness of an individual.[14] According to Hakim, women generally possess more erotic capital than men because they put more effort into cultivating it.[15] She encourages women to harness and utilize their erotic capital, especially in a patriarchal society. However, some sociologists have critiqued Hakim's concept for assuming that all women have equal access to erotic capital, regardless of race or class, and for overlooking the power dynamics that can make attractiveness become oppressive or coercive.[16]

To further refine this concept, Dana Kaplan and Eva Illouz introduced the concept of sexual capital in their work on the sexualization of culture. They differentiated sexual capital into four types: sexual capital by default (which is defined by a woman's chastity/virginity), sexual capital as a surplus body of the value (the type of capital generated through sexual labor), embodied sexual capital (the idea that "sex sells" and some people are left out of this market), and neoliberal sexual capital (some sexual recreation may translate into feelings of social competence that helps in the workplace).[17] Kaplan and Illouz's third concept of embodied sexual capital aligns with Hakim's definition of erotic capital. I redefine this idea of embodied erotic or sexual capital as femininity capital for women and masculinity capital for men within a heteronormative system of gender and sexuality. However, men's masculine value in relation to other men within the hierarchy of men depends on the femininity capital they can access.

Women's aesthetic, reproductive, intimate, emotional, and sexual labor all combine to create femininity capital. For example, heterosexual women's aesthetic labor—such as maintaining their appearance—is crucial for being valued by both men and society. Beyond aesthetic labor, men also expect substantial emotional labor from women as well. In 2016, Erin Rodgers coined the term "emotional gold digger" to describe heterosexual men's reliance on women's labor as a best friend, lover, coach, career advisor, stylist, and emotional cheerleader in intimate relationships, which coincides with Jane Ward's description of women's expected role within heterosexual relationships.[18] Heterosexual men are so dependent on women's various forms of labor that they are much more likely to remarry after divorce and studies show consistently that marriage produces good health outcomes for men and poor ones for women.[19] Most divorces are initiated by women who are fed up with their husband's lack of labor in the household; this common phenomenon is known as the Walkaway Wife Syndrome.[20]

Marxist feminist scholars argue that reproductive labor lies at the heart of women's oppression, especially for women of color, as this labor is often unpaid, considered unskilled, and frequently unrecognized as legitimate work.[21] In order to create femininity capital, women need to labor in particular ways to be coded as feminine. I am utilizing ideas of labor that previous sociologists have applied to informal and formal labor markets that highlight the gendered nature of labor that goes into creating femininity. Reproductive labor includes tasks such as cleaning, preparing and serving food, providing childcare, laundering clothes, and most importantly offering care and emotional support for families and communities.[22] Historically, reproductive labor has been associated with femininity, and this gendered division of labor within the home reinforces gendered divisions in the broader labor market.[23] As a result, jobs that involve reproductive labor, such as domestic work and caregiving, are often low-wage positions typically held by women of color and migrant women. Gendered migration patterns and the increasing mobility of women underscore the connections between economic globalization and the commodification of caring and domestic labor.[24]

Beyond the physical care involved in reproductive labor, which sustains capitalist systems, sociologist Arlie Hochschild introduced the concept of emotional labor.[25] This concept refers to the work that individuals put into managing their emotions and the emotions of others in the formal workplace. Emotional labor includes activities such as smiling, maintaining a positive attitude, and displaying appropriate emotional responses in order to meet the expectations of the job. Physical appearance also plays a role in emotional labor. Ashley Mears defined aesthetic labor as a component of emotional labor, discussing it as the work that models do to maintain their physical appearance in order to conform to industry standards of beauty and to appeal to consumers.[26] For Mears, aesthetic labor involves activities such as dieting, exercise, grooming, and cosmetic treatments, as well as managing one's image and personal branding. As part of emotional labor, the aesthetic labor of adhering to workplace beauty standards places additional demands on employees.

There are numerous motivations behind beautification practices, especially for women. Some sociologists refer to this form of labor as "beauty work" instead of "aesthetic labor."[27] Megan Rivers-Moore theorizes that the labor of being beautiful has value, is something that circulates, can be exchanged, and is relational.[28] Beauty is sold by sex workers to men sex tourist clients, who want to be seen with a beautiful woman in order to boost themselves within the hierarchy of other men. Rivers Moore finds that what drives the sex tour industry versus local red light district sex work in Costa Rica is the intangible, but highly coveted, sense of self-esteem that men receive from dating a much younger, beautiful woman.[29]

Incorporating elements of reproductive and emotional labor, sociologists Eileen Boris and Rhacel Salazar Parreñas define intimate labor as labor that entails touch, bodily or emotional familiarity, or close observation and knowledge of a person.[30] This form of labor exists on a continuum of service and care work. By joining the terms "intimate" and "labor," Boris and Parreñas challenge the traditional separations of home from work, work from labor, and productive from nonproductive forms of labor that have characterized capitalist globalization.[31] Intimate labor connects various fields of care work (such as domestic workers, nannies, and eldercare workers) through their low pay, a reflection of intimate labor's association with women's unpaid work in the home. Within this framework, Boris, Stephanie Gilmore, and Parreñas further distinguish the concept of sexual labor from sex work in order to demonstrate that a continuum of unpaid and paid sexualized services exists, ranging from transactional sex work to girlfriend experiences to hostess labor.[32]

Boris and Parreñas situate intimate labor within both the formal and informal labor markets, making it subject to the market's ideological views on race, gender, sexuality, nationality, and other factors.[33] Because intimate labor is often associated with women's work, it is frequently devalued, reflecting the socioeconomic inequalities surrounding race, gender, nationality, and class. Intimate labor is organized into what Parreñas, Hung Cam Thai, and Rachel Silvey define as intimate industries: transnational market processes of commercial intimacy that are increasingly becoming formalized within the larger global economy.[34] Intimate industries facilitate the commodified exchange of payment for intimate labor. While the commodification of intimate labor is not new, the scope and scale of the global commodification of intimacy are new. An example of this is the international dating industry, often referred to as the "mail order bride" industry, which formalizes the exchange of money for access to women's intimate labor.

Moving toward an understanding of gender as an outcome of the labor that we perform, the concept of gender labor describes the affective and physical efforts invested in giving gender to others or in suspending self-focus to help others achieve the forms of gender recognition they desire.[35] Feminist scholar Jane Ward, in her analysis of femme and FTM (female-to-male transgender) relationships, found that emotional labor (compassion, nurturing) join with physically feminized labors (cooking, sexual services, cleaning) to contribute to the production of both queer and normative genders. The burden of gender labor falls disproportionately on feminine subjects, who are naturalized as providers of this labor as "labors of love." Scholars have noted that femme partners of FTM trans individuals often feel increased pressure to perform femininity in order to buttress their partners' masculinity.[36] In this way, Ward argues that femmes *give* gender to FTMs; thus, gender labor highlights the collective efforts that produce and sustain gender.

The desire for femininity capital extends beyond cis-gendered bodies and includes the aesthetic, intimate, emotional, and sexual labor of both trans and cis women. Sociologist Brandon Andrew Robinson's study highlights men who pursue trans women, describing men's actions as engaging in what they term "transamorous misogyny."[37] This paradoxical process involves cisgender heterosexual men defining their desires for trans women based on their contempt for all women. Robinson found that cis heterosexual men hypersexualize and hyperfeminize trans women compared to their cisgender women counterparts, noting that trans women often perform high femininity—a type of femininity that many cis women are no longer willing to perform. Men interested in dating trans women focus on gender expression and desire femininity capital, but in a way that reasserts their heteronormative and cisgender masculinity. Even if these men disdain cisgender women, they still value the femininity capital that trans women produce through their aesthetic and intimate labor. Much like the men I interviewed who complained about Western women's lack of femininity capital and aesthetic labor, Robinson finds similar rhetoric among men attracted to trans women's willingness to perform femininity labors that some cis women are no longer willing to undertake.

Economies of Gender, Race, and Intimacy

The metaphor of a marketplace is consistently used to describe the heterosexual courtship and marriage process, the value of femininity capital within an economic context.[38] Economists apply theories of scarcity, labor, and capital to the human marriage market, specifically to the sexual marketplace.[39] Social psychologists view marriage as part of a sexual economy, where women use sex as a resource for social value exchange.[40] Historically, women have traded their femininity capital to gain access to men's economic capital and resources, as in many societies women could not access property, money, inheritance, and similar assets without being married.[41] Adrienne Rich's queer critique of "compulsory heterosexuality" argues that capitalism relies on heterosexuality to sustain the economy.[42] Friedrich Engels recognized the significance of women's unpaid and unrecognized reproductive labor—such as cooking, cleaning, and laundering—in regenerating the industrial workforce for capitalists.[43] Thus, some of the labor that creates femininity capital has been integral to economic development since the early days of industrial capitalism, with reproductive labor serving as a basic input of all commodity production processes.[44]

However, not all women's labor is valued the same. Feminist scholar Evelyn Nakano Glenn demonstrated that the organization of reproductive labor often creates divisions and hierarchies among women.[45] In the late nineteenth and early twentieth century, poor and working-class women of color in the United States performed reproductive labor for their own homes and for middle-class white families. These women of color handled the dirty, heavy manual labor of cleaning and laundering, while also caring for their employers' children.[46] The outsourcing of such "dirty work" to women of color continues into the twentieth and twenty-first centuries, as reproductive labor like eldercare, domestic work, and childcare is often performed by immigrant women and women of color.[47] According to Patricia Hill Collins, white women in past centuries were able to meet society's expectations of feminine domesticity, cultivating more valued forms of femininity capital, such as beauty and gentility, by extracting Black women's reproductive and intimate labor.[48] In today's society, migrant women's labor allows wealthier women the same privileges of further developing more valued forms of femininity capital.

Beyond the racialized international division of reproductive labor, women's aesthetic labor leads to different valuations of feminine capital. Women who fit the stereotypical standard of white beauty—thin, tall, and blonde—are more highly valued by men and society in the United States. U.S. beauty standards are rooted in anti-Blackness, anti-fatness, cisheterosexism, ableism, and anti-disfiguredness.[49] Sociologist Kamala Kempadoo found that many sex tourists consider Black and brown bodies desirable and erotic, yet do not view them as potential long-term wives or domestic partners.[50] She argues that the ascribed inferiority and undesirability of Blackness, contrasted with the ascribed superiority and desirability of whiteness, demonstrate how color and race define a woman's sexual capital in the political economy of desire and the sexual marketplace.

Within the international dating industry, a clear racialized hierarchy emerges in terms of the geographic locations where romance tours are offered. For example, the company I followed, A Foreign Affair (AFA), organizes tours in Colombia, Peru, Costa Rica, Thailand, the Philippines, and Ukraine, but not in Africa. As a result, countries in Latin America, the Caribbean, Eastern Europe, and Southeast Asia serve as more than just "sexscapes"—women in these regions can also be seen as marriageable partners, not just sexual encounters. Although there are informal romance tourists traveling to Africa in search of wives and love, no commercial dating agencies cater to this particular group of men. When I asked John Adams, the owner of AFA, which countries were the most popular for tours, he told me that Ukraine is by far the most popular due to the whiteness of Ukrainian women. To John, the popularity of Ukrainian women was not about racialized hierarchies but rather the perception that white women would "blend in" more and not be identified as "mail order brides." The second most popular country for tours is the Philippines, as most of the women speak a basic level of English and are familiar with U.S. cultural norms. Thus, racial hierarchies influence the popularity of certain romance tour sites, with women from some regions being considered more "exotic" than others.

Misogyny: Denied Women's Labor and Feminine Capital

Jane Ward argues modern straight culture marks a significant departure from the historical treatment of women as property and dependents, as heterosexual relationships are now expected to be based on mutual affection and equality.[51] Given this history, men in contemporary straight culture are expected to love a population they have dehumanized for centuries, creating what Ward terms the "misogyny paradox." The misogyny paradox refers to the "cultural expectation that men should like women, even as they are socialized into a culture that normalizes men's hatred of women."[52] Ward also describes how heterosexual women must perform extensive aesthetic labor—such as waxing, shaving, dieting, and exercising—to make their bodies acceptable to men, challenging the notion that straight men "love" women's bodies when so much alteration is required to be considered attractive.

Not only are feminine women expected to perform certain forms of aesthetic, emotional, social, domestic, reproductive, and sexual labor, but they are also expected to perform these tasks with enthusiasm and care.[53] When women fail to perform these labors or express dissatisfaction with their lower status in a patriarchal system, they often face consequences ranging from social disapproval to life-threatening violence. The repercussions women face for deviating from traditional femininity are what philosopher Kate Manne defines as misogyny.[54] Manne expands the definition of misogyny beyond an individual's hatred for women, presenting it as a structural system that enforces the negative consequences for women who do not perform the labor men feel entitled to in a patriarchal society. Misogyny exists to police and enforce the unequal social roles between men and women, extracting more labor and resources from women. While many define misogyny as a failure to recognize women as human beings, Manne contends that it positions women as "human givers," who are expected to provide men with various forms of labor, admiration, moral support, and more throughout their lives. Men, therefore, rely on women in asymmetrical moral support roles, being entitled to nurturing, comfort, care, and sexual, emotional, and reproductive labor, while women are not allowed to expect the same from men.

Both Jane Ward and Kate Manne trace the origins of misogyny to heterosexual men's sense of entitlement to women's labor and femininity capital. Research on the seduction industry, also known as the pickup artist (PUA) industry, which commodifies men's access to knowledge on how to seduce women, demonstrates that men often feel entitled to women's various forms of labor and will seek external, commodified help when denied this labor.[55] Ward highlights how the seduction industry appeals to men's sense of a lost heterosexual birthright and the media-fueled expectation that any average-looking man should have access to attractive women's sexual labor. This is exemplified in the film *Shallow Hal*, where Jack Black's character, an average-looking man, believes he should have access to the most beautiful women he encounters, reflecting a fantasy world in which young and beautiful women are presented to boys and men as an entitlement.

Heteromasculinity as Extraction

The narratives surrounding men's relationships with women focus on exploiting and extracting women's labor, reinforcing the market-based logic that underpins gender and intimacy in a heteronormative society. During my time following romance tours and the international dating industry, the men I interviewed consistently framed their search for love and marriage in other countries as a form of intimate geographic arbitrage. Geographer Matthew Hayes introduces the concept of geographic arbitrage to describe expatriates from the Global North moving to the Global South as a process of leveraging their relative economic influence to live more luxurious lives.[56] The men involved in the international dating industry apply this same logic to their search for love in the Global South, equating their relative affluence with an increase in their sexual market value.

Most of the men I interviewed who participated in the international dating industry viewed their search for love and marriage abroad as an economic strategy, frequently using market-based logic and narratives to describe their intimate experiences. Scholars have noted that global constructions of love are increasingly inseparable from consumptive practices and market influences.[57] Sociologist Viviana Zelizer argues against the commonly held belief that the realms of economics and love are separate and incompatible, instead demonstrating the complex economic interactions and exchanges that occur within intimate relationships.[58] The idea that love should be the driving force behind marriage is a relatively modern concept, as marriage in the past was primarily about inheritance, political alliances, and wealth exchanges.[59]

The growing economic precarity among working- and middle-class white Western men is prompting them to adopt neoliberal economic imperatives in their intimate lives, while also discussing feminism and politically correct culture as the primary causes of Western economic decline. In a time of economic precarity, "love is only slightly less contingent than work."[60] For many in the middle class, the decline in job security means that both the workplace and the domestic sphere are increasingly challenged to provide the recognition and support that people associate with love and relationships. As men's economic positions become more precarious and America's global influence wanes, those involved in the global dating industry are increasingly inclined to adopt market-based values in their intimate lives by seeking out "upgrades" to hot, young women.

In Rachel O'Neill's study of the seduction/pickup artist community, men argued that the attractiveness their sexual partners determines the men's value and worth in the eyes of society.[61] Thus, an aspirational ethos shapes these men's embodied impulses of desire, as feminine beauty is held up as an index of masculine worth and value. While men in the seduction community described their ideal woman in terms they believed were unique, both O'Neill and Ward observed that most men participating in seduction training desired the same type of woman: young, slim, able-bodied, normatively white or an exoticized "other," with conventionally attractive features like long hair, large breasts, and a slim waist. These physical traits are associated with femininity capital, and women possessing them are seen as valuable in enhancing men's heteromasculinity among their peers.

Intimate Frontiers

The international dating industry is built on the extraction of women's labor in new locations and intimate frontiers. Women's aesthetic, sexual, intimate, and reproductive labors are essential to how men define their heteromasculinity in relation to one another. Many Western men, believing that femininity capital is scarce in their societies due to the influence of feminism, seek out new frontiers of intimacy to find women's femininity capital and labor.

Western men often travel to geographic "frontiers" considered "developing" or "less developed" to leverage their relative affluence and gain access to the labor of younger, more attractive women. Despite their varied histories, these non-Western spaces share important commonalities that make them ideal for the industry: they must be safe enough for novice Western travelers and have a large population of more "traditional" women. Sociologist Vrushali Patil argues that "webbed connectivities," or the imperial networks that link different spaces and sex/gender/sexuality regimes from the proto-colonial period to today, connect the various spaces where the international dating industry thrives, all through their distinct colonial histories.[62] By "thinking sideways," as Patil describes, which involves tracing connections across sites, I show how the international dating industry utilizes different colonial trajectories of heterosexuality and gender to provide Western men with continuing intimate frontiers where they can access and extract women's labor and femininity capital.

Global Ethnography

To collect data on men's relationships within the introduction and romance tour industry, this study employs various ethnographic methods in a global, comparative setting.[63] My entry into the international dating industry began at an open house hosted by AFA in Broward County, Florida. AFA is an international dating agency that provides online correspondence services connecting Western men to women from other regions and offers both group and individual romance tours. When I attended the open house, I participated as an observer. Despite some men assuming I was a journalist due to my presence as a white woman, the presentation proceeded as planned. John Adams, the public-facing owner of AFA, discussed romance tours as the best way to meet a potential wife and emphasized the advantages of searching for women in countries like Ukraine and the Philippines. After his sales pitch, I spoke to John about following romance tours, and he agreed to let me observe as a participant in any country I wished to visit. I decided to conduct a transnational study of the industry by visiting each region where it is prevalent: the former Soviet Union, Latin America, and Southeast Asia. In each region, I chose to follow a tour in the most popular country: Ukraine, Colombia, and the Philippines.

I conducted my initial fieldwork in Colombia in 2011, observing men as they navigated a romance tour in Medellín. After the tour, I spent time observing the daily operations of AFA's local office in Medellín. The following year, I spent four weeks in Medellín, following another tour and spending time in the local office, as well as interviewing the manager of the office in Cartagena. After four weeks in Medellín and a week in Cartagena, I joined a romance tour led by AFA in Ukraine. Ukraine is unique because it offers numerous multicity tour packages, which are unavailable in other AFA locations. The tour I observed visited Kyiv, Poltava, and Sumy, and I stayed in Kyiv for an additional three weeks after the tour ended. Following my time in Kyiv, I flew to Davao, Philippines, to participate in and observe my final romance tour for a month.

In each country, I interviewed ten to fifteen men, ten employees, and five to ten local women involved in the industry. Over the years, I expanded my data collection beyond AFA to include other international dating and matchmaking agencies, most of which are based in Ukraine, with a few in the United States. I attended several conferences dedicated to international and online dating, as well as international matchmaking, in Minsk, Belarus (2017), Miami, Florida (2018), and Kyiv, Ukraine (2019). These conferences provided opportunities to act as a participant observer, recruit interview subjects, and conduct formal and informal interviews with key members of the international dating industry. At these conferences, I interviewed numerous smaller boutique matchmakers, often based in Ukraine, as Ukraine was the center of the international dating industry until Russia's 2022 invasion.

I also attended additional AFA seminars in Baltimore, Maryland (2018), and Dallas, Texas (2019), as a participant observer, recruiting men considering joining romance tours for interviews. Based on my in-depth observations of the industry, the most interesting and theoretically rich data emerged largely from my interviews with men. Previous studies of the international dating industry focused on women's autonomy and agency in choosing to participate in the industry, and potentially migrate as brides, and the importance of class in women's choices.[64] This study is the first in-depth, empirical study of both the industry and the men who participate.

The men I interviewed ranged in age from eighteen to seventy-two, came from different parts of the country (though Texas and Florida were overrepresented), and most identified as politically conservative (with a few vocal exceptions). The majority of men I encountered on tours were white, but I met a few Latino and Black men, with Latino men often choosing to attend tours in Colombia. All the men identified as "Western" (except for a few from the Global

South), as most tour participants are American, with many Australian men attending tours in the Philippines and Western European men (from the United Kingdom, Germany, Scandinavia, and France) attending tours in Ukraine.

In addition to the data I collected from AFA and its promotional materials during the tours, I began gathering romance tour guidebooks, examining various international dating websites, interviewing other international dating agency owners, and watching YouTube videos created by these agencies. I include data from AFA and Dream Connections, as they are the largest U.S.-based dating agencies still offering romance tours. I also use two guide sites, foreignbrideguide.com and internationallovescout.com, which are marketing websites affiliated with AFA and whose owners I have interviewed.

Situating Myself

During my fieldwork, I embodied what many men saw as the problem with Western and American women: I was a single white woman in her early thirties, unmarried and childless, pursuing a graduate degree in sociology—a discipline that encourages questioning traditional values. One of the tour leaders at AFA in Ukraine warned me that, given who I was, many men might not be interested in talking to me. Despite this, I approached the participants with an open mind, willing to listen to their complaints about intimacy and dating in the United States and other Western countries. Although their views on gender, politics, and the world often differed from mine, I refrained from imposing my beliefs during our interactions. My goal was not to debate their perspectives but to understand their motivations and worldviews. As a result, I had little difficulty recruiting men for this study. They were eager for me to share their stories and motivations, hoping to challenge common misconceptions about the industry. I acknowledge that my position influenced how men responded to me, and that others might have gathered different data from the same participants based on their own positionality.

I also became acquainted with a wide range of people working in the international dating industry, from owners of large websites to local women who translated emails between women and men. Through my exploration, I realized that the industry is far from monolithic. Most of the boutique matchmakers I met in Ukraine were independent entrepreneurs, and many were women. On the other end of the spectrum, the tour providers and larger U.S.-based companies were predominantly run by men. The significant role of women's labor in translating, recruiting, and managing daily operations in local offices quickly became apparent. Beyond their direct involvement, I also noticed that the industry's profitability relies heavily on women's images and unpaid labor within dating. Consequently, I apply a theoretical lens that draws from Marxist feminism, intersectional feminism, and transnational feminism to emphasize the importance of women's labor in shaping masculinity.

Chapters

Chapter 1: "Mail Order Brides," International Dating, and Intimate Frontiers explores the historical development of the mail order bride phenomenon within the context of the United States' colonial past, emphasizing the crucial role of women's unpaid reproductive, intimate, and sexual labor in the formation of frontier spaces. In settler colonies like the United States, the colonization of frontier areas relied not only on the extraction of natural resources but also on the exploitation of women's labor and capital to reproduce the nation. This chapter traces the evolution of the international dating industry, beginning with pen pal agencies that emerged in the 1970s, primarily in Asia, particularly the Philippines, and later expanding to the internet and into regions of the former Soviet Union.

The chapter then transitions to empirical data gathered from interviews with various international dating agencies, ranging from romance tour providers to small boutique matchmakers. This analysis sheds light on the complexities of a multifaceted industry that has often been simplistically portrayed as a monolithic entity involved in human trafficking. Ultimately, the chapter demonstrates how femininity capital primarily benefits men, as the majority of large agency owners are typically men, while women's labor and capital are extracted to create value.

Chapter 2: Frontier Masculinity as Extracting Femininity Capital explores the hierarchy among heterosexual men, which is determined by the attractiveness of the women whose various forms of labor and femininity capital they can access. The more conventionally "hot" the woman, the greater the boost to a man's masculinity in the eyes of other men. Many men involved in the international dating industry expressed feelings of loneliness and frustration over their lack of access to women's labor. In response, they often embraced a "frontier" version of masculinity, venturing into new "intimate frontiers" in Southeast Asia, Eastern Europe, and Latin America to seek out women's labor and femininity capital.

The men I interviewed frequently described women in the United States and other Western countries as too materialistic, too career-oriented, and ultimately unwilling to provide the aesthetic labor of beauty and thinness. Their narratives about intimate relationships with women in their own societies centered on the perceived unwillingness of these women to prioritize and please men. This perceived scarcity of women's labor and traditional relationships in the United States, coupled with the increasing economic instability many men face in the

Global North, drives their determination to seek out women abroad who they believe will provide them with the femininity capital necessary to enhance their masculinity—a status they feel they cannot achieve through financial dominance alone.

The concept of the market heavily influences these men's understanding of femininity, their own masculinity, and their expectations of how heterosexual relationships should function. This perspective reveals how gender relationships operate like economies, where certain traits are valued more highly than others.

Chapter 3: Ukraine: The Frontier of Fantasy positions Ukraine as the epicenter of fantasy in the romance tourism and international dating industry, making it the most popular destination for tours, international dating sites, and boutique matchmaking agencies. Although the industry began in Asia, and most K-1 fiancé visas are filed in the Philippines, the allure of traditionally feminine white women in Ukraine draws the largest number of visitors. For many men involved in romance tourism, Ukraine represents a place to find the fantasy of a traditional white woman. However, it is also the location where they express the greatest distrust and fear of potential romance scams.

The primary attraction of Ukraine lies in the fantasy of accessing a white woman's aesthetic labor, particularly her beauty, as well as the reproductive and intimate labor associated with traditional marriage. Men often romanticize Ukrainian women as nonfeminist white women with more traditional values than their Western counterparts. This chapter explores the "misogyny paradox" that characterizes men's perceptions of Ukrainian women. While these women are idealized as the most beautiful and traditional, they are also viewed with suspicion as potential scammers.

Chapter 4: Colombia: The Sexualized Frontier positions Colombia as the frontier of sex, excitement, and danger, where Western men seek to extract sexual and aesthetic labor from local women. Colombia is a relatively new player in the international dating industry, as the country was considered too dangerous for tourism during the 1980s and 1990s. The association of Colombia with both sexuality and danger extends to Colombian women, with men feeling as though they are venturing into a perilous frontier in search of women's sexual labor.

An important consideration in Colombia is men's perception of race. Colombia is a multiracial society with Indigenous, European, and African roots. Medellín is known for having a more "white" population compared to coastal cities like Barranquilla and Cartagena, and men on tour often expressed a preference for women with more European features. Beyond navigating this "dangerous" terrain, men also view Colombia as a fun and sexy destination, where women are available to provide various forms of aesthetic, sexual, and intimate labor.

Chapter 5: Philippines: The Frontier of Marriage explores the Philippines as a leading destination for successful marriage migration. Filipino women represent one of the largest populations in marriage migration to the United States,

Australia, and Canada. The international dating industry also has deep roots in the Philippines, as the pen pal catalog version of the industry largely originated there. Narratives surrounding Filipino women often emphasize their "caring" labor and skills; men I interviewed frequently mentioned Filipino women's backgrounds in nursing and the significant care work they performed for their partners.

Men who felt overlooked or undervalued in their local dating markets consistently reported feeling more attractive in the Philippines, where they experienced a sense of relative affluence. This chapter examines men's perceptions of the Philippines as a postcolonial frontier for marriageable women, how poverty influences their interpretations of women's authenticity, and the narratives surrounding the accessible labor of young Filipino women. The focus on youth is particularly significant, as many men travel to the Philippines in search of women willing to accept large age gaps, sometimes as wide as forty years.

1

"Mail Order Brides," International Dating, and Intimate Frontiers

Access to women's labor plays a crucial role in establishing hierarchies of heteromasculinity. This chapter explores how gender and race have influenced the historical development of mail order matchmaking in the United States. It begins with the Jamestown colonial brides, moves on to the so-called military brides from Asia following World War II and the Korean War, and concludes with the rise of the commercialized "mail order bride" industry in the 1970s. The history of mail order marriages in the United States offers valuable insight into how men have historically extracted women's labor to elevate their masculine status within the hierarchy of heteromasculinity.

The mail order matchmaking industry relies on the extraction of women's labor in new locations and intimate contexts. Women's aesthetic, sexual, intimate, and reproductive labor often remains invisible to society as recognized "work."[1] Historically, the mail order matchmaking industry has intersected with larger settler colonial projects throughout the Americas, particularly in the United States. As the industry evolved into more accessible and commercialized formats, such as catalogs and websites, men increasingly sought to extract women's labor on a global scale.[2] Social media and the internet have heightened the stakes for men striving to enhance their status in the hierarchy of heteromasculinity by accessing attractive women's sexual and intimate labor. A recent *Psychology Today* article noted that 62 percent of all dating application users are men.[3] The international dating industry presents a new frontier of dating for men who cannot access women's labor within their home dating markets. This industry profits from the free labor of women, both from images of women online and their participation in dating men and attending romance tour events.[4] Sociologist Ashley Mears illustrated how models generate capital for nightclub promoters in VIP rooms through their aesthetic labor, as wealthy men spend money on "bottles and models" to boost their masculinity in comparison to other men.[5]

Dating agency owners and promoters profit from women's aesthetic, intimate, and emotional labor, while the women themselves receive only a fraction of the earnings from their labor, such as free entry and drinks at a nightclub for models in VIP.

Beyond profiting from the allure of a potentially "hot" wife and elevating a heterosexual man's status among his peers, the international dating industry relies on the extraction of women's intimate, aesthetic, and emotional labor at every level. Most local translators, office employees, managers, and matchmakers in the Philippines, Colombia, and Ukraine are women. Many women who work in the industry as translators and managers also create profiles on the websites to seek relationships and marriage, blurring the lines between the various forms of labor they provide. Most small boutique matchmaking agency owners are women, while larger tour companies, owned by men in the United States, partner with local matchmakers to recruit women on the ground. This chapter examines the role of women's labor in the development of the matchmaking industry, tracing its evolution from the early colonies of Jamestown to the current online "mail order bride" industry, and explores the various forms of free and commodified labor that women contribute to create a multi-billion-dollar business.

Frontiers, Brides, and the Significance of Women's Labor

Lonely, unmarried men are often viewed as a social problem because they are devalued within the hierarchy of men based on their access to women's labor. Groups of unmarried men are frequently considered dangerous and disruptive, as they may engage in gay sex, commit sexual violence against women, or cross racial boundaries in sex.[6] However, large groups of single men were often sent to colonize, explore, and settle new frontiers in the Americas, creating new spaces for intimate transgressions across racial lines.[7] State regulations surrounding these intimate transgressions consistently shifted based on the state's goals during various phases of colonial projects;[8] when white women were scarce, European men's liaisons with native women were not only tolerated but encouraged.

Frontiers have served as spaces for extracting raw materials during the expansion of the United States and many other colonial and imperial projects worldwide.[9] While we often associate extractive industries with raw materials like gold, silver, and diamonds, the frontiers in the Americas also functioned as sites for extracting women's labor. This begins with the story of La Malinche, or Doña Marina, who provided vital services—translation, intimacy, and local knowledge—to help the Spanish conquistador Hernán Cortés conquer the Aztecs, and who also bore and raised his child, the first mestizo.[10] Within these frontier spaces, women's various forms of labor—whether aesthetic, intimate, sexual, or reproductive—serve as essential resources, enabling the colonial project to persist.

In the United States, the concepts of mail order matchmaking and marrying someone without a prior meeting originated in the Jamestown colony of Virginia. The initial settlers in Jamestown were all men, composed of lesser nobility, knights, and their indentured servants. Due to the shortage of available white British women in the colony, the Virginia Company actively recruited ninety women from England, offering inducements like increased legal rights, access to property, and financial incentives.[11] The Virginia Company relied on these colonial brides' reproductive labor to ensure the colony's success by increasing and nurturing the settler population.

Historian Albert Hurtado highlights the businesses and entrepreneurial ventures that many Anglo-American settler women established during the California Gold Rush, illustrating how crucial women's commercial and reproductive labor was to the establishment of "Anglo-American hegemony in the American West." He considered this an example of intimate frontiers contributing to the development of the United States.[12] After the Civil War, many white women became widows, outnumbering men in the Eastern United States, which made the Western frontier an appealing option for these women seeking husbands.[13] At the time, these marriages and catalogs were often criticized as problematic and dangerous, similar to the contemporary perceptions of mail order brides.[14] However, the popular Western romance subgenre reimagines these relationships as romantic, depicting couples who have never met before marriage, with the woman's cross-country journey culminating in genuine love. This narrative demonstrates how heteronormative stories romanticize women's labor for men.[15]

War Brides and Imperial Frontiers

As U.S. colonial settler expansion toward the Pacific concluded in the late nineteenth century, the "frontier" shifted to overseas spaces where U.S. soldiers were deployed for various purposes, including the Roosevelt Corollary to the Monroe Doctrine, the two world wars, and numerous conflicts against the spread of Communism during the Cold War.[16] After World War II, many military officers began bringing back wives from Europe and Asia, creating a new global frontier for interracial marriages. At the time, the public expressed hesitation regarding American soldiers marrying brides from abroad, leading to several bureaucratic hurdles for these marriages. The 1924 Immigration Act prohibited all immigration from Asia, and the 1945 War Brides Act did not include exceptions for women from Asia.[17]

Asian women, primarily brides from Japan and Korea, migrated through special acts of Congress that created limited windows for legal migration with their husbands. It was not until 1952 that new laws permitted the immigration of Asian wives. By 1964, members of the U.S. State Department began advocating for a "more humane policy toward Asian immigrants" in response to the increasing number of war brides arriving in the United States.[18] Discussions about Asian military spouses bolstered arguments for ending immigration quotas for Asian countries. The 1965 Immigration and Nationality Act officially abolished national origin quotas and emphasized the importance of family reunification in U.S. immigration policy, a principle that remains in place today.

In 1986, Congress passed the Immigration Marriage Fraud Amendments to prevent Asian women from supposedly exploiting American men for access to U.S. citizenship through marriage. This law imposed a two-year conditional residency period during which migrants had to remain married to their spouses.[19] In 1990, lawmakers amended the law to allow abused migrants to self-petition for citizenship before fulfilling the two-year conditional residency requirement.[20] Following the high-profile murders of brides from the Philippines and Kyrgyzstan by their American husbands in Washington state, a bipartisan bill regulating the international dating industry passed both chambers of Congress as part of the reauthorization of the Violence Against Women Act and was signed into law in 2005.[21]

The International Marriage Broker Regulation Act (IMBRA) was part of a broader anti-human trafficking policy aimed at protecting women perceived as vulnerable to abuse. IMBRA limits American spouses to filing two K-1 fiancé visas in a lifetime, with applications required to be filed at least two years apart. The law defines marriage brokers as dating agencies that charge men but not women to participate, meaning that domestic dating sites charging both genders, like Match.com, fall outside its jurisdiction. Brokers must provide women participants with the criminal and marital background of any men who contact them online.[22] Although the industry initially opposed the legislation, over time it has helped marriage broker agencies ensure that all communication occurs through their channels, providing a safety assurance and enhancing profits.

From Pen Pals to Romance Tours

In the new globalized economy, intimate industries that commodify primarily women's labor are growing and increasingly integrating into the formal economy.[23] These new economic frontiers of intimacy include virtual relationships, online dating, professional cuddling, and the international dating industry. The contemporary industry we associate with the term "mail order bride" began in Asia during the 1970s, utilizing paper catalogs and pen pal relationships to expand new avenues of intimacy for many American men uninterested in feminist women. Early pen pal companies in the United States were established by couples who actively participated in their clients' courtship processes. The catalogs, websites, and romance tours rely on the free labor of women interested in dating foreign men to generate profit; women's aesthetic, intimate, emotional, and potential sexual labor sustain the industry. The beauty of women's photo-graphs adds value, as does their emotional labor as pen pals.

The first catalog services, such as *Cherry Blossoms*, were founded by couples interested in helping Western men connect with women in Asia. Jerry Broussard, a former professor at Everett Community College in Washington with a PhD in sociology, and his wife Kelly Pomeroy began the *Cherry Blossoms* catalog as a pen pal service by selling women's addresses and later their photographs. The Flor-ences, a couple who met through a catalog service, founded American Asian Worldwide Services and vetted women's backgrounds for an additional fee from the men.[24]

The fall of the Soviet Union in 1992 shifted the industry's focus to new geo-graphic locations in addition to Asia. Another couple, David Besuden from Kentucky and his Russian wife Elena, launched Anastasia International as a specialized tour operator, taking large groups of American men to Moscow and St. Petersburg and eventually expanding to Ukraine. In 1998, Anastasia transi-tioned from paper catalogs to an online messaging format, and in 2007, the company expanded its reach by launching sister websites AmoLatina, Asian-Beauties, and AfricaBeauties. In 2011, a private investor purchased the company, relocated its headquarters to Malta, and rebranded the sites as AnastasiaDate. By 2013, Anastasia's chief communications officer, Larry Cervantes, reported that the website had over 4 million members in 110 countries.[25]

With the fall of the Soviet Union and the rise of the internet, the matchmak-ing and correspondence model shifted to online platforms, where posting women's photos alongside their addresses became easier. A Foreign Affair (AFA) began on February 10, 1996, as the world's first internet-only agency, meaning AFA never used the paper catalog method. The agency consistently employed online email correspondence and organized romance tours featuring social par-ties. Initially, AFA primarily operated in Russia and Ukraine. Unlike earlier pen pal agencies, AFA was founded by three men based in Arizona, all of whom even-tually married Russian women. The main public-facing owner, John Adams, explained that countries in the former USSR held a dangerous allure during the 1990s: "Back then in '95 [1995], that was right when, um, the Soviet Union was kind of changing. They were going through everything. The wall [had] just fallen. I mean, all this stuff was going on and things were getting more open. Um, but it was still very much kind of sexy and dangerous and different and all this stuff and Russian women are beautiful." The beauty of Russian women provided a new "frontier" for matchmaking and dating businesses to extract the value of women's aesthetic labor.

In the early days of the agency, John's partner personally recruited local women in Russia by placing advertisements in St. Petersburg newspapers and holding seminars for interested women. The international dating industry attracts men by providing access to beautiful women's aesthetic, emotional, intimate, and potentially sexual labor, as long as they are willing to travel abroad. The industry profits from using women's images on their websites, but John explained to me that agencies provide women with increased safety and vetting services that are not available on dating applications, like Tinder.[26]

> Women, when they use the service, they're getting a level of support that they can never get from a Tinder app or something like that. Right? So, they're getting a buffer, they're getting security, they're getting assistance, especially with foreign cultures, foreign language, all that. And so, it's a different level of service, like a premium service compared to a Plenty of Fish [app/website], where you just put yourself out there and you're on your own and you're gonna deal with everything, you know, this way, you know, our offices or affiliates deal with everything.

John believes that the website offers much more safety for women than during the early 1990s, which he describes as the "Wild West" of doing business in Russia. Initially, AFA sold addresses and phone numbers, but John thinks the current iteration of the industry provides women with improved safety precautions.

The international dating industry capitalizes on the economic differences between Western and non-Western countries. However, not every non-Western country offers the right mix of available single women, safety, and modern amenities for inexperienced travelers. John explained that potential tour locations must have attractive women who struggle to find life partners in their societies: "You look at fun places to go, attractive women, women that actually are finding it difficult where they live to find a life partner for whatever reason, whether it's economic, whether it's cultural or whatever the reasons are, why they would be more attracted to the Western men." On the other hand, the international dating industry does not work in similar cultural and economic settings in the West, "Like if we went to the UK, went to England, okay. It's not that much of a difference. I mean, the women are not gonna be as, 'Oh you are a guy from the U.S.' And the culture isn't that much of a difference, for the men in the UK are, are basically Western. They're treating the women pretty much the same way men here would treat the women." Ultimately, John argues that the quality of men in non-Western countries is what makes Western men more attractive, "But if you go to someplace like Colombia, um, the men there there's that whole culture of that machismo and, and then whatnot. And there is a marked difference between that and what Western men are like."

According to John, the key to a successful tour location is the availability of single, beautiful women and a "fun" environment: "The big part of it too is it's [the tour] gotta be fun. It's gotta be a cool place to go and more and more, and when I talk to guys, when I do the seminars, when we talk, I'm talking more and more about the whole social experience." Local women staff at each tour site facilitate a smooth and effortless experience for male clients, providing advice, translation, matchmaking services, and emotional labor throughout the dating process. John highlights the local staff's labor in making men feel like VIPs.

> It's just a great way to travel. I mean, where else can you go, where you just land and you're picked up at the airport, you're taken to a good hotel. You're given the low down of the surrounding area. The staff is there. You have a hospitality suite you can walk into any time during your tour, again, any help logistically that you need, or you need for dates. Great. They'll give you dates. Then the dates are taking you out, showing you the places, um, through the eyes of a local, instead of like being a tourist.

The entire experience of VIP treatment during a vacation in an "exotic" locale with available women to date is a crucial selling point for the tours. As John explains, "You're gonna have a wonderful vacation. You're gonna have an experience. You're gonna go see things that most Americans never see. You're gonna experience the food, the culture, the different people, all this stuff. Even [meeting] the [other] men on the tour, the staff you're gonna be very well taken care of, it'll be a vacation of a lifetime." This statement also highlights that many Americans do not travel abroad; approximately 20 percent of the men I met while following the industry had never traveled internationally before booking a romance tour with AFA.

Ultimately, John points out that access to younger, more attractive women is a primary draw for the industry, along with the fun of traveling abroad: "You know, it's about going over and having one of the best vacations you're ever gonna have. Having an amazing experience, meeting lots and lots of different women who tell us that they're interested in possible serious relationships and marriage, and having, I think a much better population of women from which to choose than what you might be able to find in your local city." The median age of most men participating in the industry is around fifty-three years old, and John speaks to the invisibility that many men I interviewed felt about attracting younger women in the United States:

> If you're a 45, 50, 60-year-old man, and you go to some of the singles events here [in the United States], it's a little depressing. I mean, I've been to them and it's difficult. It's hard to find [a woman]. Especially if you're say a 45 to 50-year-old guy who still wants to have a child and you go to some of these things, it's next to impossible. So, you know, I think it [the industry] gives you another option. I think it gives you just a better shot to make that happen.

Many men I interviewed expressed feelings of invisibility to the younger, more attractive women they desired in their local dating markets in the United States. They appreciated the acceptance of larger age gaps in other countries.

Contextualizing the Larger Industry

The international dating market is often viewed as a subset of the larger online dating market and has been rebranded within the industry as the Premium International Dating (PID) market. At several iDate conferences, I met Mark Brooks, a longtime consultant for many online and international dating companies. Mark began his journey into international matchmaking and online dating by working with AnastasiaDate, the largest provider of online dating services globally. Initially hesitant to join the industry and travel to Russia, he found the business model employed by AnastasiaDate to be an intriguing challenge and decided to work as a consultant for the company.

> It was like, okay, well, I got nothing to lose. Let's give it a shot. I go behind the Iron Curtain and learn more about this business. So, I did. I learned a lot more about the business and about the nature of the agency-led business that they had. I think it's changed now because they've had to change. They've had to morph. I think there's some motivation that certainly the conclusion of my working with them, that they wanted to move on from the agency model, but they were mired with the agency model. They'd lost some of their freedoms but gained a lot of their traction because of the agency model. The challenges of the agency model is you lose control. As with any kind of franchisee or partners or agencies you work with, sometimes you lose elements of control and quality.

Mark commented on how the agency-led model that most international dating companies adopt can lead to a loss of control, as many agencies franchise and collaborate with smaller marriage agencies on the ground in each country. He also pointed out that this model does not allow for strict quality control in recruiting potential female profiles and male clients.

As a consultant, Mark approached diagnosing the strengths and weaknesses of AnastasiaDate's business model. He found that international dating agencies monetize services much better than their domestic dating application counterparts.

> I think the wonderful thing about the AnastasiaDate model is, from a business perspective, they did something else, something that the rest of the dating industry never did, and that was monetize. People who were willing to spend a lot more money get a lot more in theory. So, I mean, there's a vast minority of people that will spend a lot of money, and

dating apps do not, to assist them, provide the value or help them kind of level up and get a bit more service.

In addition to concerns about the quality of agency services, Mark found that a large potential for "scams" existed when there was no true refund policy in place to protect the men clients.

> I found that the services were fraught with the potential for abuse. And one of the things that I did when I was there is I helped lay out a refund policy. And so, if a man went on to the service and discovered that the woman that he was talking to was actually in a relationship, then he'd get a full refund of every penny that he'd ever spent with that agency, because the agency's job is to make sure, you know, that the person is single. Right. So, it's complete corruption of the expectation of the client to discover that the woman is actually in a relationship and just kind of hanging out and taking the gifts that he's sending and with no intent to ever meet.

Mark's main focus was to end the avenues of potential corruption in the services provided by agencies in order to provide a more reputable product and counter the narratives of the industry as a bunch of online scammers.

He felt that providing refunds to men who engaged with women who are not genuinely single was the key to refining the quality of the services agencies provide: "So I'm quite happy with that because that kind of rips profit back away from the agencies and away from the company and back to the individuals. Incentives drive behavior. So if you got a disincentive to allow women onto the service that are actually in a relationship, then in theory, that would help the integrity of the service, which is something I was determined to do." Originally, AnastasiaDate was AFA's main tour-providing competitor; however, they stopped providing tours some years ago. Mark points out that tours are mostly window dressing for the larger online component of the business.

> It seems like tours were always window dressing. They are not profitable. They are not really profitable enough to be worth the amount of time they take. And this is across the industry in terms of events. The general realities that we understand of events is they're window dressing. The problem with the events is they're only window dressing and not a positive. If you do excellent events, it's tough to do excellent events, especially in the singles realm. So they generally end up devolving into mediocre events and being a draw on the brand from multiple ways.

Mark's impression was that in addition to events not being that profitable for the company, most of the events were not done well enough to improve a company's reputation.

Mark discussed the future of the international dating industry at Anastasi-aDate, reflecting the increasing move toward AI within social media companies such as Meta: "They've evolved beyond AnastasiaDate and now the owner's invested and built something called Eva AI. So, he's got this notion that in the future people will have relationships with AI, which if you think about it, is a really scalable business, a really profitable business. It's pure profit." Creating relationships with AI is truly profitable, as the industry often already uses chat-bots to interact with men clients, while charging them to speak to what clients believe is a live woman. The industry's shift toward AI to replace women's emotional labor within online chatting and dating demonstrates the value of that labor to begin with; it underlies the profitability of the entire industry.

In addition to consultants, the industry utilizes affiliate marketers to spread the word about the industry and to counter narratives of scams and human trafficking to mainstream the industry. Much like Mark Brooks wanted to rebrand the international dating industry as the PID market to appeal to a more mainstream market, affiliate marketers like Caleb, whom I met during 2017 and spent years interviewing, work to legitimize the industry through their websites. Thus, Caleb wrote articles challenging narratives of the industry as a scam to promote AFA's services and occasionally Anastasia-Date's: "I think, in general, our site is very pro-international dating. And I think one of the things about internet is, the internet is forever, so you have to remember that a lot of guys hear horrific stories from 1996 and they keep believing that story. And also, I think the negatives get overblown, when the guys who are actually married and happy, they go to school, and PTA meetings and they are not on the internet." Caleb highlights the fact that many men who do not have a good experience dating abroad will characterize all women on dating sites as scammers, whereas successful men are less likely to be post-ing their experiences online. Caleb explained his role as an affiliate marketer in the following way:

> Well, as an affiliate you have to try to explain what the company offers and one thing that people do mess up on is it's pretty surprising but almost every company has slightly different terms, has slightly different. . . . They have different terms. They have different products. They there's a shock, you know, when you really get into it, two things can seem superficially pretty similar but then when you get to the nuts and bolts of it, there's some pretty substantial differences between the services, the products, the cost. And so, we try to from the point of view of affiliate mar-keting, really describe what makes the site unique, all the sites that we really promote they have like one thing that we really like about them.

Caleb worked with companies that provided tours to receive a commission for each client who ended up booking a tour.

While Caleb found that affiliate marketing could potentially be lucrative, he also told me that it was hard work to chase down his commissions from many of the companies he worked with.

> But you're so far down the revenue chain, you're completely at the whim of most of the companies, because they can decide they're just going to change the policies and particularly if they're not based in the United States. You have no way to go after them, even if they are based in the United States, you have to evaluate is it really worth your time and your money to go after them and mostly the answer's no, no, no. So given that, you know, you don't have any real power and you don't have very much control over your revenue stream and you're getting the smallest cut of the revenue possible. It's just bad, bad, and bad.

While Caleb and his business partner were able to make money as affiliate marketers, Caleb points out that he has to chase down his commission from many companies, complicating his earnings potential.

When I asked Caleb about what types of men tended to utilize his affiliate website, he described them as follows:

> I tend to think, from what I've seen, the successful guys fall into a couple of broad categories. One is guys who are really geeky, never been married or mostly never been married and often have had very few relationships. This business tends to make it easier to find a relationship because at least everybody initially sort of claims that they're looking for a relationship. And so, I think for really geeky guys who are pretty positive about life, but have never been able to quite overcome the challenges of American or Western dating, this can be pretty good deal. Also, I think sometimes you have people who have, maybe you know, the whole thing about older guys doing this. I think a lot of guys, they wake up at 50 years old, they've devoted their life, they may have been married, but they devoted their entire life to their job or either career. They've been lawyers. They've been doctors. They've been whatever and they've been pretty successful and they wake up and they realize yeah, they wrecked a marriage, they have kids who don't talk to them and they want to do it right this time and they have the money and they have the resources.

Caleb observed that many older men who focused on their careers but still wanted to have families often joined the industry in search of significantly younger women. Caleb also discussed men who have had difficulties adjusting to dating culture in the West and who are marked out as nerds.

Mark Davis, a former successful AFA client who married his Ukrainian wife after meeting on an AFA tour, launched a rival tour company primarily based in Ukraine, which later expanded to Colombia and Thailand called Dream

Connections. He calls his tours "Quest Tours," evoking the idea of frontier masculinity and the thrill of adventure, while creating new frontiers of intimacy abroad. Mark cites John Eldredge's book on masculinity and femininity to emphasize that men have three fundamental desires: a battle to fight, an adventure to live, and a beauty to rescue. In his own book, Mark writes, "The pursuit of love through international dating is a grand quest that combines battle, adventure, and the pursuit of beauty—all wrapped into one. It can bring your heart to life and make you feel fully alive."[27]

As a relative newcomer to the industry, Mark does more promotional work through YouTube and blogging to get his business out there. During his YouTube videos, Mark covers a variety of topics surrounding masculinity and femininity in the West, the role of romance in men's lives, and how to be a man that women desire. He defines his YouTube channel as a form of men's ministry, all while advertising his services as more authentic than correspondence-based websites. He utilizes platforms like YouTube in order to attract a younger male clientele: "My average age [for male clients] is 38 to 40. I have been intentional from day one to attract a new generation because I really believe this was something that was falling away. I think it was appealing more and more only to guys in their fifties, sixties, and above. And so, from the beginning . . . I was 42 when I met my wife and I really wanted to market to younger guys." Mark considers men in their forties to be more competitive and successful in their search for love abroad, which ultimately helps the success of his brand. Based on this focus, Mark limits how much he works with men older than sixty.

> And I don't take guys on tours with very few exceptions who are over 60 because they're not going to be successful. I get a guy who's 62 and our average age is 38, he's going to look even older than he is by contrast and his chances diminish. And I'm not here just to take your guys' money. So, what we do is called the individual quest to our program for those guys. And we've had many marriages with guys in his sixties. But honestly my oldest client is 65.

By denying clients over sixty years old, Mark increases his success rates. He claims that 80 percent of men who attend his tours start some sort of relationship (how long those relationships last is another statistic).

When I discussed the class positions of his tour clients, Mark informed me that the average salary of his tour participants is around $70,000 annually. This salary is slightly higher than the median annual U.S. salary, but is not wealthy or even upper middle class, but he attributes that to his clients' younger ages.

> Yeah, the average income is still probably around $70,000 a year. So, I mean, these aren't rich elites, although I've gotten some guys, one guy to $17,000,000,000 net worth, and these kinds of things where I've got an

actor from Australia who can't date locally because everybody knows his face, but mostly they're regular people. I mean, I get the engineers, a lot of engineers. I don't know why I get everything from graphic designers, and accounting to small business owners. It really is just sort of a cross-breed of men. And again, if you're targeting men in their thirties, mid-forties, typically they're not multi-gazillionaires by that age.

He differentiates his business model from AFA by railing against the legitimacy of correspondence-based relationships and the websites engaged in them, but AFA also consistently tells men to go in person and not just write to women as "keyboard Romeos."

However, one major difference in their setup model is that Mark's assigned translators for men do more personal assistant labor than AFA translators. As Mark describes it, the role of the woman translator is the best friend, dating coach, and personal assistant, combining many forms of women's intimate and emotional labor.

> The second thing for me that was critically important was everybody gets a personal assistant, for the week and the experience. So, everybody's assigned a translator and it's somebody who's their best friend that's there advocating, somebody who can tell the girls, I know this guy. I can vouch for him. He's a good guy. Somebody who helps the guy by saying, look, this time, you should probably bring flowers, you should probably buy candies and different things that go along with that. And then to read the dates afterward, they spend 20 minutes afterward and they go, OK, I think this is going on that's going on. And to give the guy feedback on that and it's somebody who knows the guy's story through the whole week. And so they get to know each other and she can guide him based on how she's reading the situation. The most important thing to me was to create a dedicated personal assistant relationship for each client. And she's not on the clock, it's just somebody there to be part of the week.

Based on Mark's assessment of providing a more labor-intensive product, he felt it was fair to ask for a bit higher price for the tour than other companies, "We charge $4,950, which is probably more than anybody else out there and we include some things others don't, but it is a little more labor-intensive." However, since the war in Ukraine broke out, Mark ended his Quest Tours business. Despite hosting tours in other geographic locations, he shut down his company and is now a life and masculinity coach.

Mark is not the only man who traveled abroad in search of a wife and wanted to start a business within the international dating industry. Joe Rickards started the dating agency Match Guaranty almost by accident when he went viral on YouTube for videos discussing various "scams" that women supposedly engage in within the international dating industry. Much like the other successful dating agencies started by Western men, Joe partnered with a local Ukrainian woman matchmaker (instead of starting it with a local wife) to start the agency Match Guaranty: "It's [working with a local matchmaker] a critical piece of the element of success. Now, it's just as important to have that private Ukrainian matchmaker, just as important, but without having the Western men to coach the Western men [it's not as successful]." Joe viewed his participation in the industry as a type of legacy, where he could make an impact on making the business more legitimate in his view: "I could see I could make a difference in something and I'm at the age that I'm looking for legacy. Legacy is very valuable to me, I'm looking to make my mark in this world before I leave, I have no children. God willing one, you know, I will have my own one day. But I think, you know, people have children, and they have their legacy. So anyway. And I saw a huge capital opportunity to make a difference and change the industry." Joe's entire business model is based on challenging the legitimacy of the correspondence portion of the international dating industry by calling correspondence a scam. Thus, he committed to providing men with what he calls a lifetime match guaranty to distinguish himself from other agencies and matchmakers.

After I shared my surprise that Joe was willing to provide a lifetime match guaranty in an industry that has relatively low success rates overall, Joe explained what he meant by a lifetime match guaranty and the terms that men must follow to qualify for the guaranty.

> So, we offer the industry's only lifetime match guaranty, which is a guaranty to work with him. As long he doesn't give up and he's willing to come back, he can come and meet our ladies, get unlimited meetings or dates and unlimited coaching until he gets married. Oh, yeah, terms and conditions. So, they have to fully utilize the annual package, which means they have to come four times for whatever period, but it's up to two weeks. But having said that, I would say 80% of guys that come after the first trip, they leave in a relationship that they're happy with.

Beyond requiring men to come multiple times to Ukraine in order to meet women, Joe also implements what he calls "zones of success," which include realistic expectations for men, especially in terms of age gaps: "The other big term condition is he has to stay within the zone of success. I've coined zones of success, five different points. The biggest point is the age difference, so he can't date more than 15 years [younger], or his guaranty is null and void. And so basically, if we don't see that the guy can be successful, we don't invite them to become a client." In order for Joe to provide his guaranty effectively, he vetted clients more carefully in terms of their expectations for dating younger women and their appearance.

He already considered the process of relating across cultures with Ukrainian women to present a challenge for successful long-term relationships: "And we don't know them [Ukrainian women]. We don't understand them. And they don't understand us [Western men]. I mean, I've experienced it firsthand here with, you know, a number of relationships. And it's just very difficult to bring one of these relationships to fruition that ends up in a happy marriage." For Joe, the souls of Ukrainian women are inherently different, making working with a local matchmaker an essential component of success.

Joe traced Western men's frustration with the dating market in the United States to feminism, which men often considered the basis of losing access to women's various labors in the West: "You can ask any Western man that comes, oh, say, American man, Canadian. Well, we're American, Canadian, New Zealand, and Aussies for the most part. They all say the same thing. It's like playing a broken record. They all say feminism. And they're tired of feminism and emasculation. And they want traditional values, they want a woman for whom family is the most important." Joe also hit on the fact that many Western men felt denied access to women's labor, making them feel invisible within their own dating markets: "And they have a lot of bad experiences. And that's predominantly the reason and the beauty of the women. The beauty is number one." Finally, Joe delves into the importance of women's aesthetic labor of being beautiful to highlight why men would be interested in dating women in Ukraine.

The focus men clients have within the industry on traditional heterosexual relationships and gender roles within those relationships has been well documented. However, Joe raised some concerns about Western men's ability to actually financially provide, echoing Kimberly Kay Hoang's finding that many Vietnamese women marriage migrants face gender vertigo upon migration to Western countries, as their husbands cannot provide an adequate living to sustain them in their Western home countries.[28]

> And yes, it's perceived that Western men are definitely better providers. For the most part, they are. But are they? But are they when they leave Ukraine? Because there's a total myth here that the Western people are rich, as far as Ukrainian people think. But will Kenny be a better provider when he takes you from Ukraine to America? Well, maybe not. And that's a shocker to a lot of women. I think too, when they get there.

Joe's observation regarding the assumptions that Western men will be better providers does not always pan out for women in the international dating industry, as Monica Liu observed with Chinese email order brides and their Western suitors.[29]

Ultimately, many of the agencies started by men are in tandem with either a wife or local women partners. Mark Davis from Dream Connections states that his local partners on the ground in various countries are essential for the success of getting local women to sign up with his agency: "Anytime we start a new market, we have to go find local partners because, until we have an office and get to know people, we don't have our own ladies database. And so, when we started here, Nikolaev, my wife is from Nikolaev. I met her in Nikolaev and the agency she signed up with, she was friends with the owner, so it made it very natural for us to go in there." AFA, although started by three single men on the ground in Russia, also has to affiliate with local agencies and matchmakers in order to access local women's profiles on a large scale.

John explained to me that in Ukraine, marriage agencies have become quite a strong cottage industry.

> But up in the last 10, 15 years, there's been such a seed change in Eastern Europe to where it's a cottage industry, it's a huge cottage industry and all these little marriage agencies pop up, and either you work with 'em or you don't. So, if we choose not to work with anyone, we're gonna be very limited to the number of women that we could actually make available or, you know, have available to, um, for the men to meet. Um, so it's almost like you are, you have, if you're gonna do business in Eastern Europe, you have to figure out a way to work with affiliates. Otherwise, it's just not gonna work. And it makes it a lot more difficult, I think, than it used to be when it was just us. Cause we had more control, it was our, our thing and one came to us.

Due to the popularity of Ukrainian women, and how easy it is as an American to travel there visa-free, the international dating industry has become an expansive cottage industry within Ukraine and has diversified a lot more than the industry in Colombia and the Philippines.

Matchmaking: Labor of Crafting Love

Since the majority of Western men fantasize about dating traditional white women, the industry's most innovative changes often occur in Ukraine. Many small, local boutique matchmaking agencies operate there, frequently collaborating with larger companies like AFA to share women's profiles or organize tours. With hundreds of small dating agencies in Ukraine, AFA typically partners with local agencies to recruit women across the country. Both the affiliate office and AFA share profits from emails and gift sending, and AFA features profiles of women from various local offices on its larger websites. During romance tours, AFA often collaborates with local agencies rather than establishing an office in every city where it hosts tours, as was the case in Sumy. The dating agency in Sumy, owned by a local Ukrainian woman married to a local man, had no interest in dating American men, nor did the translators who worked for her; they believed local men shared "the same mentality" as themselves. During the tour, she worked with AFA to host the social party and help men arrange dates, similar to the official AFA office in Kyiv.

Following a multicity tour in Ukraine in 2012, I returned for one of the major international dating industry conferences, iDate, in 2018 and 2019, and I also attended the same conference in Minsk, Belarus, in 2017. The iDate conference brings together various stakeholders in the online dating industry—including tour providers, matchmakers, affiliate marketers, and payment processing companies—to share information and network. In addition to smaller affiliate dating agencies, like the one I observed in Sumy, I met several high-end boutique matchmaking agencies at the iDate Conference, including Possible by Natali Koval, For Him Dating, and Prime Matchmaking. Unlike romance tours, where men receive introductions to women through social events and dates, the matchmaking industry in Ukraine adheres to the traditional definition of matchmaking.

The media and previous scholarship often depict the industry as one where men profit from the images of women or even from their direct trafficking.[30] However, in the cottage matchmaking industry that has developed in Ukraine, many local Ukrainian women dominate the field and choose to affiliate with larger agencies like AFA. These matchmakers do not use the correspondence model typical of international dating; instead, they focus on in-person interactions. They work with clients willing to travel to Ukraine to meet women selected from their databases based on compatibility. In the summer of 2019, I collaborated closely with Natali, the owner of Possible, to understand the differences between matchmakers and companies focused on tours and correspondence. Natali had approached me the previous year at the iDate conference and was genuinely interested in a scientific perspective on love, dating, and courtship. She invited me to observe the daily operations of her office, where she and two other women assisted both male and female clients. The first step for both genders is to fill out an intake form detailing their interests, educational background, and personality. Natali's office featured several books on matchmaking, psychology, and personality types, and she has a background in psychology herself.

Natali has been doing matchmaking since her university student days, working part-time with international dating agencies: "I don't know what they paid, but it was a lot of money then. It was like super cool. Super cool job. Yeah. Especially for a student. Right. So plus, you're dealing with foreigners so they make it all interesting, and all the restaurants, you know, like different places. And I was curious, you know, and that leads me throughout life and gives me lots of energy." Initially, Natali worked as a translator, advising men on dating Ukrainian women. After getting married and having her first child, she began freelancing as a translator, directing men to various agencies and engaging in early forms of matchmaking. Eventually, she decided to invest in her own agency by purchasing an office. In addition to matchmaking, Natali offers relationship coaching, U.S. fiancé visa support, image consulting, and wedding planning services in Ukraine.

Natali and her employees provide men with essential emotional support, as searching for love can be a time-consuming and emotionally charged experience. Unlike many international dating agencies, they do not use a correspondence model. Instead, they work with clients who are willing to travel to Ukraine and meet women selected from their database based on compatibility.

Natali has more older female clients than AFA, as local AFA agencies require express permission from the Arizona office to add women over forty to their sites. Most of Natali's clients are in their early thirties and generally successful in their careers. In Ukraine, women over twenty-five are often considered "over the hill" in terms of marriageability. While I observed the office, Natali hosted a special workshop with a female psychologist who examined different personality types and their compatibility in romantic relationships. About fifteen women packed into the small office to hear the psychologist's advice and ask questions about relationship compatibility. Most attendees were in their early thirties and successful in their careers. Viewed as too old by local standards, these women sought Western partners but often worried about leaving their successful careers in Ukraine behind.

Many women at Natali's agency spoke English and were genuinely hoping to find men who were interested in serious relationships. When I asked Natali what her main advice to women at her dating agency is, she replied,

> Don't expect Prince Charming with a ton of money. So, look for more than just money. And I would tell her that when you're meeting a guy, treat him as if he's your classmate that you haven't seen for 10, 15, 20 years, that you haven't seen for a long time, somebody you've known, somebody who was not as like strangers, and talk to him. Talk to him openly, like treat him as if he's not a foreigner, as if he is coming from Ukraine from like a closed circle.

While most of Natali's matchmaking efforts focus on Western men, she also works with professional Ukrainian men. However, many women enter the industry with dreams of young, wealthy Western men who will romantically sweep them off their feet, a notion reflected in Natali's main piece of advice.

In terms of applying scientific principles to her matchmaking, Natali often utilized sociological principles in her matchmaking, focusing on matching people with similar class and educational backgrounds: "They [the couple] have to be in a similar economic status, well not in exact figures, right? But middle-class figures to their [respective] cultures and their education and what they both want out of a relationship." In terms of advice she gave to men, Natali always told them to be careful with spending a lot of money early on in the relationship.

The majority of the men signed up with Natali's agency were interested in having children: "My main clients are the guys, uh, 35 to, say, 55 who still want to have kids." For women in their forties or older, it was often difficult to find a match through the industry, as many men wanted women who were significantly younger than themselves to have children. Looking at the demographic background of Natali's men clients, the median age is around fifty-two years old and most of the men in this age demographic are searching for women in their thirties, if not younger.

Beyond Natali's work within her own matchmaking agency, she partnered with her colleague Alex, a boutique matchmaking agency owner based in Poltava, to create the Ukrainian Matchmakers Alliance. They created this collaborative effort between various premium professional matchmakers to introduce best practices within the industry and improve the reputation of the industry overall. According to the Matchmakers Alliance's website, "The Matchmakers Alliance is an officially recognized legal entity in Ukraine to promote and regulate its certified Members within the national matchmaking market best practices and conduct."[31] As of right now, the alliance works with fifteen different matchmaking companies in a variety of Ukrainian cities, including Kyiv, Poltava, Odesa, Mykolaiv, and Rivne.

During the 2019 iDate conference in Kyiv, Natali and her partner Alex provided an introductory seminar before the main conference on Ukrainian family values. Natali began by discussing the importance of family and marriage in Ukrainian culture: "Number 1: You marry once, you marry for all your life, stay married together and you grow as partners, you grow as a family and you marry for life. The next thing is we stay close as families, we support our families, and our family means a lot to us." After highlighting the importance of the family, including the extended family, Natali and Alex began to discuss the importance of traditional gender roles within the family and the importance of men taking on the role of financial providers.

Natali then started talking about the importance of men taking on the provider roles within the family by earning more money and how Ukrainian women not only liked that but expected it within their marriages.

> Here in Ukraine women want to put the biggest financial responsibilities on the man's shoulder. They are looking for a man who is financially responsible, who is capable of supporting the family financially, and who is able to let her be the mother, be the housekeeper at least for some time. Not all of them want to be housekeepers. They are okay with letting the job wait, be in charge of the family, help kids grow, help them to at least get to school. But the man then has to understand that if she is not achieving in her career, then she needs some resources. So basically, in a good Ukrainian traditional family, men give money to the women and say

"I don't care where you spend it, for dresses, for fun or for taking kids out, for getting gifts for your family."

Natali further explained to the other matchmakers and members of the industry that women in Ukraine are happy with men who take on the traditional role of male provider: "And I see that in Ukraine women are actually happy to be financially dependent on the guy. They don't think it's something bad, they don't think this is something to be ashamed of. They are okay with it and most of them are happy to be financially dependent on a guy in a good way."

Another member of the Ukrainian Matchmakers Alliance is Elena, the lead dating coach and owner of Prime Matchmaking Company, a boutique agency based in Odesa, Ukraine. Like Natali, Elena brings a strong professional background to matchmaking, having completed numerous certifications in the field. She works with a team of women, including trained psychologists and other matchmakers. Rather than featuring a database of available women, the Prime Matchmaking Company website highlights the roles and credentials of its employees in facilitating successful romantic relationships. As a boutique agency, Prime shares fewer profile photos, similar to the approach taken by Natali's and Alex's websites, and most of its services cater to in-person clients who visit Odesa.

Elena sees love and relationships as necessary for both men and women to feel complete and satisfied in life: "I came to the simplest, like all ingenious, conclusion: in the modern world, at least in our and Western countries, with our mentality there is no other reason to be a couple other than love, common values, interests, when [in] the lives of both you are much better and of better quality than alone!" Elena's perception of contemporary heterosexual relationships recalls the notion of the "pure relationship" from sociologist Anthony Giddens, who argued that heterosexual relationships are increasingly entered into for love and common values versus economic necessity.[32] Based on these views, Elena sees her role as a matchmaker to guide and help both men and women find love with compatible partners by providing coaching services and blogs and videos to her clients.

The paradox of the industry is that Western men participating are seeking more traditional women, while women participating are often seeking more open-minded men.[33] Elena explains on her website to the women clients that foreign men do not want a maid and are more helpful when it comes to completing the reproductive labor of the home.[34]

Foreign men do not expect that someone will clean for them or wash the dishes, because they don't think that it is only a woman who should clean up. Home duties there are not divided into male and female. They really appreciate their wives. For Western men, it's okay to go for a walk with the baby and let his wife rest. They love their women and do not want to load them with extra work. When he has free time, he will certainly offer his help.

Of course, this quote is ironic, as most of the men participating in the international dating industry are looking for women who are still willing to perform the reproductive labor of the home, but these more conservative men are portrayed by agencies as being more egalitarian than local men in Ukraine (in this particular instance).

Alex, Natali's partner in starting the Ukrainian Matchmakers Alliance, follows the typical narrative of a Western man who married a Ukrainian woman and started an agency after opting to stay in Ukraine. Alex left Portugal, moved to the smaller city of Poltava with his wife, and started a boutique matchmaking agency. During his component of their presentation at iDate 2019, Alex agreed with Natali about the importance of men taking the lead in relationships.

> For a wife you need to be the mother; for a husband you need to be the head of the family. The head of the family is the guy that has the capacity to bring home the economic power, so the family is happy and has the minimum good conditions of life. That is our responsibility, and that the wife is not too worried because she is making your life easier, taking the kids to school, taking care of the house and preparing everything for everyone in the family.

While women in Ukraine work, the main responsibility of providing for the family falls to the husband, who is supposed to be the economic power within the family. Here, Alex is characterizing marriages in terms of the common idea of gendered labor exchange; women exchange their reproductive labor for financially being cared for. Furthering his explanation, Alex highlights again the importance of men taking the lead within the family structure: "Hopefully we [men] take charge. It is something like, a Ukrainian woman is like if they like the man, it doesn't that much matter exactly what is the plan. She will be happy to follow." Alex wrapped up by pointing to the popularity of those traditional gender values and how they are not as common in Western countries anymore.

Many men attempt to stay in Ukraine and live the expatriate life, and many have a dream of starting their own international dating agency. Alex was one of the rare men who successfully started a local agency in Ukraine, with a successful long-term marriage and business. The majority of matchmakers and local agency owners are women in Ukraine, so Alex based his matchmaking agency on relating to men, as he had once been a Western man looking for a wife in Ukraine. He largely traced his success to understanding his men clients.

> Because I am here [in Ukraine] for 13 years, I know how they [Ukrainians] think; I live among them. I know the culture very well and I, on the other hand, I'm also a foreigner, so I know the difficulties that they [men clients] face because I faced the same. Right, so I can tell the main advantage has to be with knowing exactly how the culture is and how they

operate and their mindset. Being a foreigner from my perspective looking to the culture, third I'm a man like them so I speak to them, "cut the
shit off." It's like, man to man, I do not have the politeness of a translator
or a woman that coaches now, I'm foul. I'm a bro here. I'm ready so pay
me to speak the language that they understand, to say the shit as it is and
they say "yes, Alex. Give me the shit. I pay you to give me the shit."

Alex's blunt communication style with his men clients was indeed very different from the softer approach utilized by many of the women matchmakers I met,
including Natali. I saw throughout the various times I observed Alex that he
developed very close friendships with a number of his clients, catering to their
various whims. For example, he was invited to stay with his clients in the United
States as a friend and guest.

Alex was convinced that men became addicted to finding Slavic women
after they came to visit Ukraine, and he confessed that he was one of the men
addicted: "There's nothing like when you drink this blessed water from the Slavic
girls, you don't want another. You will never adapt to anything anymore. I would
never ever marry a European, no way. So there's a kind of phenomenon. That's
why these guys come eleven, twelve, twenty times, because many of them, they
like the process." Many of the men I interviewed throughout the tour experience
commented that even if they did not find marriage, they enjoyed the large
amount of attention they received from beautiful women in Ukraine and felt
more invigorated by this attention.

Alex further explained to me that Ukrainian women do not need to use sexual labor, their aesthetic labor is enough to drive men crazy.

They [Slavic women] don't need to lay down. Oh, that's why I say these
ones are the most difficult to get in terms of Slavic girls, Ukrainians
are very difficult. Not only by the level of intelligence, scholarships they
have, and the mentality they have underneath, it's only in their favor and
they know how to manage that very well because they are educated
since children aged 2 to push the value of the woman up because their
beauty is their biggest weapon. My daughter six years of age, she was
already going to school with painted nails and lipstick.

In Alex's opinion, Ukrainian women's greatest weapon is their beauty, an important form of aesthetic labor that society encourages from a young age, as even
young girls wear makeup and nail polish. Based on the cultural expectation of
aesthetic labor and beauty, Alex argued that Ukrainian men became spoiled and
were likely to cheat: "They [Ukrainian women] serve their beauty, [it] is their biggest advantage, but at the same time because the guys choose them by the
beauty, they [local men] can have the best girl in town. But if you eat fish every
day, you get annoyed by the fish and suddenly you can eat even rotten meat,

at least well because it's different." Much like the rest of the industry, Alex took a traditional viewpoint on masculinity and men's need for multiple sexual partners so they do not get bored.

When I asked Alex why he thought online dating and international dating has grown so much in the past few decades, he traced the growth of the industry to people's increasing loneliness in late capitalist societies: "People gamble online, people see more online, people make games online and people date online. It is another hobby for the loneliness of many Americans. They know that dating Ukrainian women is out of their league. But for them to fulfill their egos to receive letters that they associate with a beauty and it makes them feel happy." Alex's comment also points to the importance of associating with a beautiful woman as a way to provide heterosexual men with a boost to their sense of masculinity, highlighting the importance of women's aesthetic labor in defining heterosexual men's position within the hierarchy of other heterosexual men.

All of the matchmakers within the alliance, and those outside the alliance as well, focused on cultivating relationships based on similar interests and personalities, in addition to looks. They played a much more direct role in their men and women clients' relationships but also charged more money for their personalized services. In Alex's estimation, too many agencies were trying to make a quick buck through emails and correspondence instead of investing in real matchmaking services and higher-end clientele with more money to spend. He wanted to start the Ukrainian Matchmakers Alliance with Natali to bring a certain level of regulation to the industry to combat the stigma that the entire industry is a scam: "Yes, I started the alliance to try to find some reputation for everybody. But I will have several difficult processes because everybody wants and I cannot accept them because if I put the rotten apple in, then clients will post bad about all of us." Thus, creating the alliance acts as a form of quality control that helps all of the member agencies create positive profiles and feedback.

I did meet with one boutique agency owner in Medellín, Colombia, but the preponderance of boutique matchmakers in Colombia was not as prevalent as the cottage industry in Ukraine. I interviewed the owner of an agency focused on serving a more financially well-off clientele. When I asked Michael about how he got involved in the industry, he explained how he foresaw Colombia's tourist boom coming when he visited to meet women.

> So, four or five of my friends have moved out of the U.S. since I did. I came in 2007 to Cartagena originally. I had businesses and I was looking to do something different, and I knew Colombia was coming up. I had a lot of Colombian employees in NYC [New York City], and I knew it was hot and it was happening. I actually got involved with one of these dating websites, Colombian Cupid, which I am sure you know. That is our big competition. What happened was, I met some girls and I was interested in

coming. I was not scared to come, I have been all over the world and traveled to 81 countries. I was going to meet this girl in Trinidad or somewhere they can go since a lot of places they need visas. So, she couldn't travel. So, it was Christmas Eve, and I was like I will come and boom. And I got here, and I got to be honest with you, I saw it right away. I have been in Africa and Europe when it was really starting to move, you could see this was coming. It wasn't ready, so I went back and kicked around for a year, sold my business, and I had to stay for six months more and I just came. I took one year and traveled around, took opportunities, I met people, because you here you have to be really up. Like tomorrow, I have lunch with a senator. You can have lunch with congressmen, senators. If you are honest, and you do what you say you can do, anyone will see you at any time.

Michael referred to his connections, both business and political, as an important component of setting up any type of business abroad.

He explained to me that he started dating local women upon his arrival in Colombia and felt empowered by the attention from women: "I had just gotten to Medellín and I had broken up with another girl before I came who I had been with for a long time and I was dating, dating, dating and it was so much fun. You know why? When you're American, you can date anyone. You are in a different place. And it was great." Despite feeling privileged as an American man when accessing Colombian women's intimate labor during his dating spree, Michael felt that while many of the local women are fabulous, they are unsophisticated: "It was great for awhile and then I started to get a little bit bored of it. And I went on to Badu, which is another website. So, you could just sign up with a picture and the emails would just flow. So, I was looking for something very specific, which she [his Colombian wife] understands. I love these people, but they are not sophisticated." However, he met his wife Juliana who had traveled before and seemed to him to be more sophisticated than the other Colombian women he dated.

As a New Yorker, Michael had been married twice before to women in the United States, but both were Latina women, Venezuelan and Colombian. When I asked him what he liked about Latin women, he responded, "The hair is the first thing. I like that they have good passion to them. And like I said, I don't like to sound really Freudian but they're women like I remember growing up. And I don't think I'm sexist at all, I really don't." To further demonstrate his non-sexism, Michael explained that he often worked with women: "I have partners that are women. To me, woman or man, it doesn't matter what you do. To me, I like the way that they are women. I have friends, where never ever have we had anything together and with Latin women, I just have a great rapport with them." In addition to seeing economic opportunities in Colombia for the international dating industry, Michael traced his interest in the area to his love of Latin women. Based on his attraction to Latin women, Michael explained that his friends felt empowered in the Colombia dating market versus their home dating market in the United States: "My American friends around me went crazy. They have girlfriends here and other girlfriends in from Peru. It's when you first get here. It is different since for your whole life it was a challenge. And then it's less challenging." Similar to many of the men I interviewed, Michael found dating in the United States to be a challenge, whereas he considered dating in Medellín to be easy.

Michael caters his services to the elite end of the client spectrum, focusing on providing high-end services that many other companies providing tours do not provide.

> The tourists, the people, they are just coming. You are losing money every single day that you don't do this. And what happened was we are still in a position here where people are like still a little scared of Colombia. We bring them in and we greet them at the airport. You get in and you go to a private apartment, it's not a hotel. We have apartments that are spectacular, with gifts and a fruit basket, you have everything you asked for and your robe, your slippers. We then take them to a number of different things, El Pinole, Santa Fe Antioquia. We have different sorts of get-togethers: toga parties or cocktail hours and you can come or you can not come, whatever you want to do. We book plane tickets, we book all your ground trip needs. You pay one thing and you don't pay again unless you go outside of what we are doing. Saturday night we have a huge party at the *finca* [farm]. You sleep over or you can come back if you want. You have taxi service available all night. We have a transport company as well. You stay there all night, you hang out at the pool, surf, there are waiters and waitresses and the whole thing.

Ultimately, rather than focusing on gaining a little bit of money from several clients, Michael wanted to focus completely on capturing high-end business men as clients, similar to Alex's mindset in Ukraine. He characterized his clients as more happy: "I want to work with people that are happy. That's what want to do. Just want to work with people that are happy. This has always been my thing. And we think this is probably a 5 to 10 million dollars a year business. Which is pretty good." Michael was still in the early stages of developing his matchmaking agency but was focused entirely on attracting higher-end clientele and providing them with very personalized services.

If Michael could not access wealthy clients, he wanted to work with men from the U.S. Midwest, whom he also characterized as less sophisticated people: "My target is actually the Midwestern guys. They are a little less sophisticated about it, they still have money to do it with, they find it exciting. Midwestern and Western guys always are a little more adventurous than city guys, who are hard to deal with. I either want the really rich ones or the normal guys from the rest of America." Michael also did not want to deal with younger guys who were only interested in coming to Colombia for partying and sex: "So I am not looking for the 25-year-old kid who wants to come here to snort cocaine and have a party week. I'm looking for adults that want to come in. We are very much boutique-y. Ten clients a week maybe maximum, maybe a little bit more. Usually, they'll come in to date specific girls but we introduce them around." Michael ultimately characterized rural Colombians and Americans as both unsophisticated

Despite discussing his avoidance of young party-oriented clients, Michael did mention that partying was still a major component of the services he provided to his clientele.

> But we bring the party along with you. Our Saturday night parties are incredible, they start in the afternoon and you can come out whenever you want, as you always have transportation. We start on Saturday night and we serve appetizers and that kind of thing. They will cut a roast beef or something. I'm kind of chefy myself. Then they party all night, then they go back into town for the discos or whatever, we take them back because it's like 20 minutes away or they stay through the night until Sunday, because you know what happens on Sunday here? On Sunday, nobody moves. They are all hammered and hung over. So, we let them do that. When it's warmer weather, in the morning you go into the pool and you hang out, there's music, we BBQ all day and we have waiters/waitresses, the whole thing. Leave when you want, come when you want. Do what you want to do. That's a little respite because then on Monday we have them starting the tours to Pinole and Santa Fe [smaller cities near Medellín], so we will be getting into Zona Cafeteria [area of Colombia known for coffee growing] pretty quickly. We just want to see how the first ones go before we do that with them because it's a big long ride. It could be six hours to Armenia [city in the Zona Cafeteria].

Michael's services also included travel to other areas in Antioquia, such as the Zona Cafeteria and Santa Fe, that were arranged and coordinated through his agency to provide the most personalized services possible.

Ultimately, Michael saw his role with the boutique matchmaking agency as promoting the growth of the local economy in Colombia.

> We want to sell this country. We are here to promote the country; I am meeting with a senator tomorrow. First, we go through this company, and they realize what they have for tourism and what can happen with tourism. Colombia has the potential of a Hawaii or whatever you want to

say, but it's so much closer. We think we can leverage that. We think
that there's enough people who haven't been here yet that they will want
to come and explore and see what's going on. And you know, even with
the things happening in Cartagena with the secret service, all the press
has been good for us. We are trying to take advantage of that and that's
why we are moving things up pretty quickly.

In his other business roles, Michael saw the economy of Colombia rapidly developing with large numbers of increasing tourists. Tourism has only continued to
grow in the past decade within Colombia and particularly Medellín. With the
large growth in tourism, there has also been a concurrent growth in crime
targeting tourists. At the end of 2023, eight Americans utilizing various dating
applications ended up murdered, targeted by gangs that utilize dating applications to meet foreign men for theft.

Intimate Markets and Women's Labor

The majority of intimate industries, or industries that commodify various forms
of intimate labor, like call centers and sex work, are inherently extractive.[35] As
sociologist Arlie Hochschild and journalist Barbara Ehrenreich argued, care
labor has become the new gold in a globalizing economy.[36] These forms of labor
are often categorized as "women's work," and intimate industries are typically
dominated by female workers. The international dating industry is one such intimate industry, relying on the extraction of women's labor in various "frontier"
spaces. The foundation of the entire international dating industry is the access
it provides to younger women's aesthetic and intimate labor for men who feel
they cannot obtain similar services in their local dating markets.

   As the extraction of women's labor is integral to the construction of heteromasculinity, the international dating industry has grown steadily since the 1970s,
in part as a response to men's backlash against feminism and its push for greater
equality in intimate relationships. Feminism's call for equality in the home creates barriers for men seeking access to various forms of women's labor. The
industry contends that Western women no longer compete with each other in
terms of aesthetic labor, leading to a perceived decline in maintaining a feminine appearance (e.g., high heels versus sneakers). Additionally, Western women
are often portrayed as so career-focused that they are unwilling to provide emotional, reproductive, and intimate labor to men. Many of the men I interviewed
expressed nostalgia for the family life of their childhoods, where stay-at-home
moms were fully dedicated to their families.

   Like traditional matchmaking operations, the international dating industry offers men access to women's labor that is unavailable locally. Most of the
men involved in the industry are not wealthy or even upper middle class; they

are seeking intimate frontiers where their money has more influence. For many, having financial resources is a key factor in attracting an attractive woman for dating or marriage. When traveling abroad, middle-class American men find that their relative wealth increases their appeal to the younger, more attractive women they struggle to find in the United States. Thus, the industry profits from the various forms of labor women provide throughout the process, from the aesthetic labor of their photos to the emotional efforts of matchmakers and the intimate and reproductive labor provided by girlfriends and wives.

2

Frontier Masculinity as Extracting Femininity Capital

Throughout my decade of following the international dating industry, the men I met frequently expressed feelings of invisibility within U.S. society, particularly in the dating market, especially if they were over fifty. These men often had unsuccessful relationships and marriages with local women and believed that feminism had prevented them from accessing the labor of younger, more attractive women, which they felt entitled to.

As feminist philosopher Kate Manne argued in her book *Down Girl*, misogyny should be understood as the hostility and violence that women and girls face daily, which serve to enforce and police gender norms and expectations.[1] Misogyny goes beyond individual feelings of dislike or hatred toward women; it acts as the policing mechanism of patriarchy, keeping women aligned with certain gendered expectations. Manne highlights that women are often expected to be "human givers," providing traditionally feminine goods—such as sex, care, nurturing, and reproductive labor—to designated, often more privileged men.[2] Conversely, women are expected to refrain from taking traditionally masculine goods—such as power, authority, and claims to knowledge—away from men. These goods are tacitly deemed the entitlement of privileged men, and this illegitimate sense of male entitlement gives rise to a wide range of misogynistic behaviors. According to Manne, when women fail to provide what men believe they are owed, they are punished for this perceived transgression. Men involved in the international dating industry often framed their loneliness within narratives of entitlement to the labor of younger, "hotter" women.

Men on these tours frequently described dating in the West as difficult for the average man, arguing that women have all the choices and options in the dating market. Nikola, from the introduction of this book, explained that money is the most important component of sexual market value (SMV) and can often outweigh looks: "Yeah, SMV is more than looks. SMV includes money, status, reputation, and the famous 666 . . . 6-inch dick, 6-figure salary, and 6 feet tall. So, knowing SMV includes all that . . . the only thing that works is money to get the hotties. Once you cross over into wealthy, looks don't matter as much." Sociologist Beth Montemurro examines the role of accessing sex from women as a defining feature of the hierarchy among heterosexual men and found that many of her interviewees define hegemonic men in the sexual marketplace similarly to Nikola: tall, financially well-off, good-looking, athletic, and able-bodied.[3]

The contradiction in men's complaints about women's increased choice and selectivity in the dating market lies in their often rigid criteria, primarily seeking conventionally attractive, "hot" women. The number one fear for heterosexual men using online dating is that the woman they meet will be heavier in person than in her photos. A pervasive discourse on dating apps includes calling women "fat" or "not hot enough" when they reject men's advances or do not respond to messages.[4] Jane Ward considers these moments as examples of the misogyny paradox at play since men lash out in misogynistic ways after being denied access to women's intimate and sexual labor.[5] Sexual rejection is a significant blow to men's masculinity, and accessing the most attractive women possible, or "trophies," is a crucial component of fitting into the hierarchy of heteromasculinity.[6] Beth Montemurro found that "hot" women served as currency in this hierarchy, boosting the average heterosexual man's masculine status among other men. Many of the men Montemurro interviewed were also frustrated by their lack of access to "hot" women, demonstrating that the views expressed by men participating in the international dating industry or the seduction coaching industry are not as marginal or fringe as some may think.[7]

Beth Montemurro's work underscores the role that sex with women, especially "hot" women, plays in men's understanding of their masculinity, particularly in relation to other men. Women's labor and femininity capital thus become building blocks of masculinity, as men focus on accessing women's sexual and aesthetic labor when comparing themselves to other men. As discussed in chapter 1, the international dating industry acts as a "middleman," connecting men from the United States with women in other countries who are more likely to engage in the types of aesthetic, intimate, and reproductive labor that many women in the United States are no longer interested in performing. When heterosexual men cannot access women's various forms of labor and feminine capital, they describe feeling invisible and emasculated, highlighting the importance of women's labor in defining heteromasculinity.

Frontier Masculinity

As American and other Western women increasingly expect equality within heterosexual relationships, a growing subpopulation of men in these countries are resisting these expectations and turning to the internet and online international dating services to broaden their search for intimacy.[8] Global markets of intimacy have given rise to various intimate industries that provide different forms of intimate forms of labor within the formal economy to men.[9] The international dating industry, in particular, offers a new "intimate frontier" for men who feel denied access to women's labor in their home countries. The concepts of frontiers, exploration, adventure, and empire are deeply gendered, with men often envisioned as explorers and frontiersmen venturing into the unknown in search of wealth and glory.[10] Men interested in expanding their search for intimate relationships beyond national frontiers existed throughout U.S. history, as discussed in the previous chapter.[11] However, increased global connectivities and media representations like *90 Day Fiancé* are normalizing cross-cultural relationships and the development of the "passport bro" movement.

The scholar Scott Melzer argues in his book that "frontier masculinity" animates men involved in the National Rifle Association movement.[12] He describes frontier masculinity as characterized by rugged individualism, hard work, protecting and providing for families, and self-reliance. Melzer considers contemporary frontier masculinity a descendant of a mythologized version of manhood rooted in the United States' frontier past. Historian Gail Bederman examines the development of manliness at the turn of the twentieth century as a response to social changes, evolving expectations of womanhood, and racial anxieties surrounding non-white men. She highlights Teddy Roosevelt's advocacy of manliness to illustrate how the closing of the Western frontier in the United States fueled concerns about American men becoming too "soft" and the need for middle-class white men to reassert their manliness in the face of challenges from racialized men.[13]

The men involved in the international dating industry often see themselves as part of a cultural minority within the United States, feeling judged for their frontier masculinity and conservative views on heterosexual relationships and gender roles. In a scholarly article published in 2021, I discussed how similar conservative views of gender norms within heterosexual relationships animate the international dating industry and various online communities of men reacting to feminism, such as men's rights activists, the seduction community, incels, and Men Going Their Own Way.[14] Kate Manne notes that incels are not just angry but aggrieved; not just disappointed but resentful. They feel entitled to the labor that women are expected to provide in their asymmetric support roles. As feminism has challenged many discourses surrounding women's unequal roles within heterosexual relationships and families, men in these communities have vocally rejected the idea of egalitarian heterosexual relationships. The men I interviewed also felt largely ignored and lonely within their local dating markets and saw the international dating industry as a space where they could exert frontier masculinity in their intimate lives by seeking to marry more "traditional" women and be recognized as "good guys" with value. Thus, these new frontiers of intimacy created by global intimate industries offer Western men access to women from whom they believe they can extract labor and feminine capital, in contrast to their perceived inability to do so with Western women due to feminism.

Failed Relationships and Loneliness

Discussions of late capitalism highlight the loneliness that increasingly characterizes many Western societies, where social ties have significantly weakened in the past fifty years.[15] In his famous book *Bowling Alone*, political scientist Robert Putnam argues that various factors, such as television and suburbanization, have contributed to the decline of social capital—our connections to others in society.[16] Loneliness is on the rise in the United States, with former U.S. Surgeon General Vivek Murthy even calling it a "growing health epidemic."[17] Feminist scholar Eleanor Wilkinson critiques the equation of loneliness with being alone and the positioning of loneliness as simply an individual feeling or emotion.[18] In a neoliberal framework that emphasizes individualized solutions to social problems, individuals are often held accountable for their perceived failures to create social bonds and are labeled as such, like incels or the stereotypical "crazy cat lady." One individualized solution some men are adopting to cope with loneliness in Western societies is to purchase women's aesthetic, intimate, emotional, and sexual labor through intimate industries such as sex work or international dating.

I met Canadian Rick in Natali's office in Kyiv. He had attended a romance tour with Mark Davis's Dream Connections and then decided to utilize the more personalized services of a matchmaker and he found Natali through recommendations. Rick was not in search of a "hot young woman"; instead, he was disillusioned by the demands for gender equality within heterosexual relationships in Canada. He explained that many Western men are frustrated with their local dating options due to women's increasing expectations for equality: "So for that reason, the rational reasoning, I think, you know, a lot of Western guys want the whole family thing—it's, you know, the gender equality. Not that I'm against that, but it's not what I'm looking for." Having devoted his youth to building his business, Rick felt he was missing something important in life as he approached fifty. "So, for me, turning 50 was the big deal. You know, they always say men have a midlife crisis. I work hard, I've worked in corporate. I started my own business for the past 10 years; I haven't had time to really dedicate myself to a serious relationship. So, when I turned 50, I was like, okay, I have success in my business life, but I'm missing a big part of my personal life." Entering his fifties, Rick realized he wanted a family in addition to financial security.

Rick was a successful businessman, owning real estate in Canada, and had delayed marriage and family life to focus on his business goals. Now that he had more time and money, he wanted to start a family and have children. Since women within his age cohort typically cannot have children biologically, Rick believed his only option was to find a younger woman who could still have children. However, finding someone at fifty to start a family with proved challenging: "Now I'm like 50, and of course women around my age bracket are married, divorced, and don't want to or already have children. I'd like to have a family. So, for me, it is necessary to have a younger wife, you know, late thirties." Many of the men I met during tours who were looking for significantly younger women justified their desires by expressing a wish to have biological children.

Rick also complained that many Western women are only interested in older men if they are extremely wealthy, a sentiment shared by many of the men I interviewed. "And so typically, that's [a large age difference] a no-go unless the guy is super wealthy, like Hugh Hefner's wealth, which is not me. Western women are not typically interested in older men." Although Rick was financially well-off, he did not consider himself wealthy enough to attract younger women in his local dating market. However, he believed he had a better chance in Ukraine, where he felt a slight cultural connection. "Where this is more common is Eastern Europe, and my godparents are from Ukraine, so I had a small connection, a little bit of a custom. So that's how I did the whole Ukrainian research thing to begin with. So that's why I came for a potential Ukrainian wife."

Unlike Rick, who had never married or had children, Derrick had been happily married for twenty years before losing his wife to cancer. Together, they had raised three grown children, but he still felt lonely without a partner to share his daily life. Derrick described his life as empty without his wife and kids at home: "I have this nice house, but it's empty and too quiet." He began searching on domestic dating sites like eHarmony.com, but found the women too geographically distant, and on Match.com, where he felt the women were "creepy." Disappointed with his local dating options, Derrick expanded his search to international dating sites and chose AFA because it seemed legitimate. As a religious man, Derrick's main criterion was a shared faith: "For me, as long as my wife believes in God and going to church, that's the most important." Based on his religious principles, Derrick opted to forgo the tour experience and instead communicated with one woman in the Philippines via email for a long time before traveling to meet her in person.

Many of the men I spoke with had experienced difficult relationships and divorces, often attributing their dissatisfaction to Western women, particularly American women, not providing the type of labor they sought. I met Greg, a fifty-five-year-old overweight realtor, during a romance tour in Colombia, and he shared the story of his first marriage's breakdown with an American woman, who was also the mother of his children. "I think we just grew apart. The last five years [of the marriage], she wanted to stay home, and I wanted to go. You know, if there was a party, I wanted to go or a show I wanted to go to, and she would stay home on the computer. She had a couple of internet affairs, and my daughters knew about it, and I didn't. Finally, I found out about it. It was a good excuse to say, hey, you know, I'm out of here." After the marriage ended, Greg raised his children and felt that his daughters still resented their mother for the breakup. "I mean, they have their relationships with their mom, but I still think they have a little bit of resentment." Greg was disappointed that his wife had emotional affairs online during the latter part of their marriage and no longer wanted to participate in activities together.

Despite his sadness over the end of his marriage and his wife's internet affairs, Greg eventually found his second wife, a Russian woman, online. "Met her [second wife] on the internet and went over to Russia. You know, I just went to see my wife in Russia; I didn't go to a party like these [the AFA social parties]. I didn't go meet a whole bunch of Russian women or do the dating and the partying and all that. I just dated her. I probably talked to her for eight or twelve months on the internet before I went over there." However, Greg's marriage with the Russian woman also ended in divorce, much sooner than his first marriage.

Greg encountered numerous problems, especially with his Russian wife's disdain for most Americans. "We had a good time together, but there were some red flags that I should have noticed. Like when we were in Rome, we were supposed to share a cab with some people from America who were staying at the same hotel. She just said, 'I don't want to go with them. I just want to go with you.' I told her, 'We're just riding downtown with them; it's only a ten-minute ride.' But she insisted, 'Nope, I'm not going.'" Her reluctance to interact with Americans did not stop there—she had little interest in hanging out with Greg's friends or making new American acquaintances. "She just wasn't pleasant to other people. When she was with her Russian friends, she was happy-go-lucky and sweet," Greg shared. As a very social person, Greg grew miserable in the relationship, exacerbated by conflicts with his new stepson, whom he described as poorly behaved. "I didn't really spend much time with the kid; he was a brat," Greg added. By the time we met, Greg was dating an American doctor who had given him a "hall pass" (an agreement to have an "open" relationship for a short period) so he could attend the romance tour in Colombia, which he had already booked before they started dating.

However, Greg's new American girlfriend did not meet his expectations for feminine appearance—she was too casual in her look. "I mean my girlfriend here [in the United States], she's not a girly girl, she's pretty but she doesn't do a lot of makeup and she's a doctor and you know when we go out she wears jeans most of the time. She owns a motorcycle; she's just not as, you know, she's not girly girl." On the other hand, Greg found his second Russian ex-wife and women in Colombia much more attentive to their physical appearance; for example, he described his Russian wife as being "drop-dead beautiful." For Greg, a woman's aesthetic labor in performing femininity was a crucial factor that encouraged him to join AFA romance tours.

I met Daniel, a forty-eight-year-old HVAC business owner from the Midwest, on tour in the Philippines. He too felt disappointed by his first marriage to an American woman. After some medical issues, Daniel's wife no longer felt like having sex with him, denying him her sexual labor. Daniel explained to me that sex is an important component of a successful intimate relationship: "Basically, my wife was having some medical problems and she refused to take hormone replacements. And this basically killed her sex drive. Like nothing. It was like I have absolutely no desire for that. And that's an important part of a relationship." As Montemurro demonstrated, men's access to women's sexual labor is an important aspect of their masculine identity. Daniel gave his wife three years to figure out a solution, but when she still did not show interest in sex, he decided to end the marriage. "So I gave her three years, and it wasn't working. We're still good friends, and I would do anything for her, but she had to decide what she wanted to do." With no change in his wife's sexual desire, they decided to end the marriage, remain friends, and co-parent their teenage daughter responsibly.

I met Adam randomly at a restaurant in Kyiv while conducting a different interview with an affiliate marketer for the industry. He overheard our conversation and wanted to share his story. Adam began by highlighting the loneliness that drives many men to seek intimate relationships abroad. "I think there are several reasons [to pursue relationships abroad]. One, if you're feeling low, if your self-esteem isn't great. Maybe you're not having any luck in your own country, or like my friend, you're just feeling down. He happened to be there, and it happens—you feel low." Adam argued that another major reason men come to places like Ukraine is their search for sex work. "You see all these pretty girls, and to be honest, there are so many sex tourists here [in Kyiv]." Adam identified himself as part of the first group, traveling to Ukraine in search of romance after a failed engagement back home. "I suppose I fell into the sad category if I'm being honest. I had been engaged at home, and it was the one that broke my heart—after breaking a couple of hearts. It was like God saying, 'You know, it's your turn to feel it.'" He continued, telling me that they called off the wedding, and he was single for a few years afterward. "So, we broke off the marriage date and blah, blah, blah. I was genuinely on my own for a couple of years."

During Adam's single period, a friend introduced him to the idea of dating women from the former Soviet region. "A friend of mine who worked in Eastern Europe had a girlfriend in Russia, another in Ukraine—he used to take all these girls to Turkey on his yacht, his hired yacht. And he was an absolute sex tourist. But he kept saying, 'Adam, come to Ukraine, come to Russia.'" For years, Adam declined his friend's invitations. "I kept saying for two years, 'I'm not interested; that life isn't for me. They just want something from me.' Those were my thoughts then, but they definitely changed later—oh, very much so." However, after meeting his friend's girlfriend, Adam quickly changed his mind about visiting Ukraine. "She [the Ukrainian girlfriend] walked in, and I said, 'Okay, I'm coming to Ukraine,' because she was stunning. I had never even considered it before. So, long story short, I went on the websites." Though not ready for a serious relationship, Adam saw traveling to Ukraine as a way to "get back in the game" without facing as much potential rejection as he would in his hometown.

Taylor, divorced and in his mid-fifties, from a rural Midwestern town, was in Kyiv and hired Natali as a private matchmaker. One of his main concerns was a woman's weight, as his wife had gained weight during their marriage. "I guess I accepted my wife the way she was [overweight]. First of all, I was happy to find her and that she accepted me for who I am. She was a pretty sharp-looking lady when she was younger. But when she had our daughter, she put on a lot of weight and got pretty heavy. Every time I tried to help her figure out something to control her weight, she got mad at me." Taylor was disappointed by his wife's weight gain, and his main criterion for dating Ukrainian women was finding someone with a thin body frame. Despite his frustration with his wife's weight gain, he saw them as partners working together to survive financially in their home.

In addition to Taylor's frustration with his wife's weight gain, he also became frustrated with her spending habits, feeling they did not earn enough as a couple to support her expenses. "Well, finally, she realized she was just as responsible for the money in the divorce as she was when we were together. I think she thought she could just bail from it [their mutual debt]." Taylor assumed that his wife was trying to escape their shared debt, and based on this assumption, he had trouble trusting new intimate partners. "I try not to get angry. I was never a jealous person before, but that changed me. It's really hard to trust, but I'm getting better at it now." As his marriage began to fail, Taylor focused on work. "My release from all of it [relationship issues] was working. I worked my butt off, kind of putting my frustrations into my work, and I had a tough time with that." Taylor also struggled with the downgrade in his living situation after the divorce. "All of a sudden, I went from four acres down to an apartment. So, I had nothing to do, just sitting around, bored. I had to learn to relax, settle down, and enjoy. It's still hard for me to live in an apartment because we lost our house to foreclosure and bankruptcy. I went through bankruptcy, foreclosure, divorce, and a new job all within three months." After his bad luck with both finances and romance, Taylor struggled with dating in his small rural town, especially since he was looking for a woman willing to put in the aesthetic labor to maintain a thin body—a rare find in his Midwestern town.

Nikola, from the introduction of the book, identifies as an introvert and focuses on earning as much money as possible to achieve his goal of leaving the United States to move to Ukraine. When discussing his dating history, he always emphasized the importance of money. "Even with my first job, the first thing I spent my paycheck on was taking a girl out to dinner. Without money, you can't invite a girl on a date." Nikola had dated women of various races in the United States, but was haunted by the rejection of a stereotypical hot blonde woman. The failures and rejections he faced in his local dating market led Nikola to embrace the red pill ideology, which argues that Western society is now stacked against men in favor of women, and that women are only interested in hypergamy, or "marrying up" in wealth.

Nikola embraced this ideology by avoiding serious relationships with women in the United States and focusing on work and earning money, echoing libertarian ideals that the United States still offers many opportunities to those willing to work hard: "My point is this. People in the USA are poor because they choose to be. This is the one country where you can achieve your goals. Can't say the same for any other country but people don't have the right mindset to break through their own fabricated glass ceilings. I myself have that problem with women but not with money or career but I admit that I am a prisoner of my own mind with women. Too much pain endured in the past holds me back from trying but not in money and career." The pain from rejection in the past colored Nikola's attempts at having real intimate relationships with women in his local dating market and even at times abroad. He complained to me about his experiences on romance tours and using Ukrainian matchmakers like Natali as well. One issue he had with the more conservative dating culture in Ukraine was the lack of physical intimacy Ukrainian women were willing to provide on dates, providing a different type of frustration in access to women's labor and femininity capital.

The stories of the men I have shared here highlight the loneliness and resentment toward Western women that often drove them to participate in the international dating industry. This loneliness and resentment frequently stemmed from their inability to access the labor or femininity capital they desired from the type of high-value women they felt entitled to. Many men complained about disappointing relationships with women in the West—women who no longer provided the aesthetic labor of maintaining thin bodies and feminine appearances, the sexual labor of being available for sex, or the reproductive labor of prioritizing family over careers. They often blamed their lack of access to these forms of labor on feminism, which they believed had shifted gender roles in society and encouraged women to move away from the traditional labors associated with femininity capital.

Changing Gender Roles and Decline in Access to Women's Labor

Friedrich Engels highlighted the crucial role that men's extraction of women's unpaid reproductive labor—such as cleaning, cooking, and laundering—played in sustaining capitalist systems.[19] Over the past thirty years, some sociologists and cultural theorists have argued that heterosexuality is moving toward more egalitarian and democratic ideals, often referred to as a "pure relationship."[20] However, feminist sociologists continue to show that men still participate significantly less in household reproductive labor than women, leading to what is known as the "second shift."[21] That pattern has not changed dramatically in the past thirty years, leading many feminists to consider the feminist revolution to be "stalled."[22] As long as gender inequalities persist institutionally within society, true gender equality cannot exist within heterosexual relationships.[23]

Heterosexuality, and heterosexual men in general, remain dependent on the extraction of women's labor in various forms. Based on the gendered labor gap within the home, increasing numbers of middle- and upper-class couples outsource the reproductive labor of the home to migrant women and women of color, such as domestic work, eldercare, and childcare.[24] With the expansion of global markets, further outsourcing of intimate labor is increasing, and this labor encompasses a range of activities, which include maintenance of bodies and households and the family, as well as sexual contact.[25] The variety of commodified forms of intimate labor available within intimate industries are gendered as feminine and affordable.[26]

Several intimate industries cater to men clients, as men define their masculinity through access to women.[27] Sociologist Raewyn Connell defines gender as relational, showing how masculinity is always constructed in relation to a feminine other, within a framework of hegemonic masculinity and emphasized femininity.[28] Judith Butler highlights the role of heterosexual desire in reinforcing a hierarchical gender binary through the concept of the heterosexual matrix, a hegemonic discursive model that assumes a stable sex must be expressed through a stable gender, which is both oppositionally and hierarchically defined through compulsory heterosexuality.[29] Numerous scholars of masculinity have demonstrated that heterosexual desire often forms the basis of men's masculine identities.[30]

Sociologists have documented Western men's attempts to "buttress" their masculinity through utilizing industries that commodify the intimate, sexual, and aesthetic labor of "other" women, such as the sexual tourism industry, the romance tourism industry, and hostess clubs.[31] Research on the seduction industry, which commodifies men's access to knowledge regarding how to seduce women, shows that men often feel entitled to "hot" women's various forms of labor and seek external help when they are denied it.[32] Early scholarship on the international dating industry considered it another form of outsourcing reproductive and sexual labor to migrant women, underscoring the significant role that access to women's labor plays in defining masculinity.[33]

In Rick's view, marriage and family life are far from the minds of Western women, and he explained, "But that's the reality, you know wanting a wife who is happy being a wife and mother and my experience with a lot of Western women is like that's the furthest thing from your mind." Rick blamed the advent of feminism for the lack of accessible women interested in performing various forms of labor in the service of men, relationships, and families in Western countries: "So in general I just, I don't know. It's [feminism] a bad thing in that it's contributing to the disappearance of the traditional family values and traditional family model." Rick's story echoed those of many other men who waited until they had achieved professional success before seeking marriage and children, only to find that young, fertile, and attractive women were no longer accessible to them in the West.

Eli was on his fourth tour in Ukraine when we met. He attributed his dissatisfaction with dating in the United States to shifting gender roles and expectations. To Eli, it was "natural" for men to want to engage in masculine behaviors and to desire women who engaged in feminine behaviors. However, he believed the opposite was happening in the United States. "The reality is men want women to be women, right? I don't want to marry a woman who wants to be a man because who's going to be better at it, me or her? On the flip side, in the U.S., there are some gender issues and role issues, and really, you have men acting like women and vice versa," he explained. Echoing Mark Davis's idea that we live in a "gender-confused" culture in the West, Eli believed that women no longer act feminine, which puts him in competition with them, making it more difficult to benefit from their labor.

I met Mitch on his eleventh trip to Colombia. He had fallen in love with the country, partly because of its proximity to Boca Raton, Florida, where he lived. Mitch agreed with Eli that the changing gender norms in the United States posed serious problems for men in relationships. "Women in South America, Asia, all over there, the man comes first. We see a clear definition of roles that society runs on. In the United States, our society forces women to behave like men, but here [in Colombia], it's a woman's thing to be feminine. Women in the United States have forgotten how to be women and feminine," he said. Mitch viewed places like Latin America and Asia as more traditional in their gender roles, where men are often the number one priority in a woman's life.

I have previously defined this expectation as the emotional labor of selflessness. Men's expectations for women's emotional labor highlight the asymmetrical support roles women often assume in relationships, as noted by Kate Manne in her definition of misogyny. However, Mitch did not see his expectations of being the top priority in his wife's life as misogynistic. "And I am saying that without being chauvinistic. I don't want someone at home naked cooking me dinner before I get home every night. No. But you know, I want a partner, not . . . I don't want a challenge when I get home. I have a very stressful job, and I have challenges all day long. I want a partner," Mitch explained. He viewed his desire for an "easy" relationship as incompatible with the expectations of an equal relationship.

Tom, a man in his early sixties from Texas, blamed feminism for ruining heterosexual women's relationship expectations in the United States by telling them that they could have it all. "Well, they've [American women] been told for so long that they can have everything, you know, that they can have the career, they can have the family. And then they're working on their career real hard to be successful, which everybody wants to be successful. Then they get that, and at 40, they want to start a family. It's bullshit. You've missed your window of opportunity on the way up, and now you're looking for it on the way down, and they're dating 27-year-olds while they're 45," he said. Tom's comment points to the fact that while men can focus on their careers and lead bachelor lives well into their forties, the same does not apply to women. He considered women wanting to start a family later in life to be "bullshit," believing they should have settled down when they were younger and more fertile. However, Tom did not recognize that his underlying assumption is that women's primary focus should be on the labor they can provide for potential families, particularly husbands, rather than on their careers.

Nikola, who adhered to the red pill philosophy, saw the gender norm changes influenced by feminism as detrimental not only to men but also to women: "Women today are wayyy more stressed than women back then. Because men back then [pre-1970s] men took on the stressful jobs, but women are joining those jobs now too. And the stress is getting to them. Because men were programmed for generations to handle stress. Women are recently only jumping into highly stressful jobs." In Nikola's view, women's labor of raising families and tending to the home was not stressful. He believed that women joining the workforce had increased their stress levels, making them unhappier than when they stayed at home. "Many women today are making more money but are more miserable, yet they will never accept responsibility for it. They will dodge and refuse to admit it's their own fault for taking on such jobs," Nikola argued. Like Tom, he believed that women's decision to prioritize careers over family was ultimately making them more miserable. "Feminism is not making women happier, and it's making men more miserable too," he would often tell me.

Jimmy, a fifty-six-year-old restaurateur I met on a tour in Colombia, explained to me that women in the United States are spoiled and too career-driven, challenging the traditional gender norms in heterosexual relationships that position women as providing more labor for men. "As far as my opinion of American women, as wrong as it probably is, ask anyone we know if I am wrong. They're spoiled; they are way too career-driven when they are young, and when they are older, all they want to care about is children and grandchildren," he said. Caring about children and grandchildren was uninteresting to a long-term bachelor like Jimmy, making it difficult for him to connect with women his own age in the United States. "You know, I tried dating some women my age, 50 to 55 years old, and we had nothing in common; I have no children and I certainly don't have any grandchildren, so their conversation revolves around their grandchildren, and that's all they can talk about. It just seems like they have no other interests," he explained. As a man in his fifties, Jimmy felt that men's value to women continued to decline as they aged. "I feel in America, for the most part, the man on the priority list of the woman moves way down the ladder and continues to move down the ladder as life goes on," he observed. While never directly faulting feminism for the shift in gender roles, Jimmy nonetheless was uninterested in women not willing to perform the emotional labor of selflessness or prioritizing their man.

Applying Market Logics to International Dating

For men involved in the international dating industry, dating is often framed in economic terms. Rachel O'Neill's research on the seduction community, also known as pickup artists within the manosphere, demonstrates that heterosexual men often apply market logics to dating.[34] For example, men are willing to invest in seduction bootcamps as a way to access women's intimate and sexual labors. O'Neill argues that the seduction industry perpetuates an understanding of heteromasculinity as being based on men's sexual access to women's bodies. Similarly, men in the international dating industry view dating as a marketplace, where women are assigned numerical values, typically from one to ten, based on their physical attractiveness. The aesthetic labor that women perform on international dating websites is a primary draw for men entering the industry.

Men often define their masculinity by their access to women's various forms of labor, particularly aesthetic and sexual labor, and many industries profit from women's femininity capital, including the international dating industry. Sociologist Cynthia Enloe connects the role of women's labor to the development of several industries, such as tourism (from flight attendants to sex workers), militarism, and the global economy.[35] The value of women's aesthetic labor is essential to a number of industries, including the nightclub industry. Sociologist Ashley Mears, in her study of VIP rooms in nightclubs, demonstrates that promoters and clubs rely on the presence of attractive models to make money.[36] However, the models themselves gain very few direct benefits, apart from free alcohol. In the international dating industry, women's sexualized images generate profits, but their aesthetic labor rarely benefits them personally.[37]

I met Peter, a Jewish man in his fifties originally from New York, who had moved to Boca Raton, Florida. He was on a tour in Colombia with his good friend Mitch. Peter described his dating experience in Boca Raton negatively but felt he had more choices in Colombia, a situation he compared to how women experience dating in the United States. He explained, "The analysis that I see is what attractive American women go through on a daily basis, being inundated by men when they go to a bar. That's what I am experiencing here. It's different. Like there [in the United States], they [women] can say, 'I don't like this one, I get to choose.' I have the ability to choose here." Having faced rejection in the United States, Peter considered himself considerate and polite when rejecting women in Colombia. He explained, "Since I have gotten the other side of that at home, I am not rude about it here." Peter wanted to show empathy to women he rejected, which he felt was often lacking when women rejected him in the United States.

Peter frequently compared his increased choice in women during his trip to Colombia to what women in the United States experience daily. "When I first came here [Medellín], my friend who lives here said, 'You're going to be like a kid in a candy store, sort of like a woman in the United States. You are really going to be inundated, looking at all the beauty, and you're not going to know what to do.'" Peter indeed felt overwhelmed by the sexual attention he received in Colombia, which boosted his masculine confidence significantly. Despite his access to various forms of labor from very young women in Colombia, Peter wanted to find a woman closer to his age, as he felt uncomfortable dating a significantly younger woman in the United States. He pondered, "Go have your fun, but when you come back a second time, you understand and go for something more realistic. Do I really want to bring home a 19-year-old to the United States and hold her hand while people stare at us in Walmart? It doesn't look good; it's not a good thing." Thus, even though the allure of younger women drew Peter to Colombia, he still wanted to adhere to a respectable age difference according to U.S. societal norms.

Dating abroad on tour is a highly formalized experience, often with a translator present during the first couple of dates for those who do not speak the same language. In this structured world of courtship, men often look for signs of physical intimacy as indicators of genuine sexual interest. Peter expected women to express some form of physical touch and felt entitled to this intimate labor, especially when he was paying for the date, if they had been out more than a few times together in order to feel the woman had genuine interest in him. He explained, "But when you are paying for dinner, drinks, and transportation, which I am happy to do, it's not a lot, but you want a little sincerity, a little more. Because if you've had two dates and haven't even gotten a hug, a touch on the back of the hand, or a thank you, do you really have any relationship?" Ultimately, Peter sought a warm and affectionate woman. "I ask myself, what do we have in common besides looks? Does she care for me? Does she grab my arm? Is she warm?" In this way, Peter viewed his search in Colombia for a potential wife as increasing his chances of finding a woman willing to perform the caring and intimate labors he found lacking in Boca Raton.

Taylor, like many men I interviewed, had difficulties finding suitable women on domestic dating sites like Match.com in his small Midwestern town. In particular, he struggled to find a thin woman and thought he could increase his chances in the Ukrainian dating market. After his experience with his ex-wife, Taylor became almost exclusively focused on finding someone thin. He shared, "My ex was a pretty heavyset lady, and I'm looking for someone who has a nice figure and dresses well. I don't want someone skin and bones either, but I want someone with a happy medium, not a really heavy person." The primary reason drawing Taylor to Ukraine was the increased aesthetic labor women there were willing to perform to keep their bodies sexually appealing and thin compared to women in his local dating market.

One of Taylor's first dates in Kyiv was disappointing, as the woman was heavier than he expected. "She was a heavier-set gal, and her pictures made her look a lot thinner. She looked very different from her picture. Awesome lady, but I want someone skinnier, not so heavyset." Despite his lack of interest in her appearance, Taylor still enjoyed the woman's company on the date and they even discussed how couples should split household responsibilities. He said, "We had a good time talking about doing dishes, laundry, responsibilities. I believe it should be split down the middle. Both of us should do it. It's not the woman's responsibility to take care of the house if she's working. It's just as much my responsibility as hers to help clean and cook." While scholars of the international dating industry consider it a form of outsourcing care and reproductive labor to migrant women, Taylor's comments highlight that most men in the industry value women's aesthetic and sexual labor more than their reproductive labor in the home.

Dale, whom I met on tour in Colombia, stood out for several reasons. Dressed like a cowboy from Texas, Dale was in his late thirties and much younger than the average tour participant. Additionally, Dale was from a lower socioeconomic stratum than most of the other men on tour. As a truck driver, Dale had to scrimp and save to afford the tour in Colombia and strategize his time off work. Dale told me he was intent on finding success on this trip, as he likely could not afford to return for another tour. A divorced father of four children, Dale expressed his desire to find a woman with children already, believing that a mother would be more understanding of his situation.

While women's reproductive labor mattered greatly to Dale in terms of helping to raise his children, Colombian women's aesthetic labor remained a significant factor in his participation in the tour. He observed, "I don't know enough about these women down here [in Colombia], but they all want to look beautiful for everything . . . they pretty much get the guys they want, you know? So that's a little scary for me because their most important thing is looking beautiful and pretty." Even though Dale desired a beautiful, femininely dressed woman, he was also intimidated by her femininity capital. He commented on the difference in people's attention to their appearance in Colombia versus the United States:

> These people care more about what they look like, and Americans aren't that way. I mean yeah there are a lot of girls that do it in the U.S., but I

think here [Medellín], cuz when we see so many [women], it's closed in where for us [U.S.], everything is spread out. But if you go in the store, you know or somewhere you see more girls down here that take care of themselves more than the U.S., I will say that. You know over here you're breaking your neck, and you just don't do that in the U.S., you know?

Like a number of other men on tour, Dale explained being in Colombia as being overwhelmed with choices in beautiful women as being "like a kid in a candy store."

I met Tanner on tour in the Philippines. He was a partially disabled veteran living in Alaska, and he explained that there were not many women in Alaska to begin with, and many of those were not interested in dating a partially disabled man. Several of his friends had married Filipina women and suggested the AFA tour to him. Like Dale, Tanner found the most beautiful, model-like women intimidating. "In all honesty, as much as I want a pretty girl, I don't want someone so far above me that I'm always trying to keep up. And I really don't want that model style because I'd be uncomfortable with that." While accessing a beautiful woman's aesthetic labor is an important component of masculinity, a few men I interviewed were intimidated by women they considered "out of their league" in terms of looks on a one-to-ten scale.

Tanner was further convinced that trophy wives who just stayed at home were often miserable since they could not truly develop a sense of self: "I hate to say it, but I'll say that a lot of guys consider trophy wives. I mean they [trophy wives] end up miserable, because you're like, 'Hey, don't do this, don't do that, don't do nothing' you know, and they don't get to . . . enrich themselves, they don't build up self-confidence through what they wanna do, through work." Ultimately Tanner felt that "taking care" of a woman left her infantilized and dependent, similar to a child. For this reason, Tanner wanted a woman interested in working outside of the home once she migrated to Alaska. He wanted her to have a sense of self outside of the home and marriage, arguing that work is what gives people self-confidence.

I met Adam on a tour in Ukraine, where he had already been on several similar trips throughout the country. Adam saw himself as a realist among dreamers, having learned the ins and outs of dating in Ukraine through his numerous experiences. He was critical of men who believed that their "Westernness" and assumed relative affluence were enough to attract educated and attractive Ukrainian women for marriage. He said, "I don't know if there's this false sense because you're [Western men] in a different country [non-Western], and you think the girl is more desperate or something, but no, that's not always the case." To Adam, Western men who assume women in non-Western countries will automatically fawn over them out of financial desperation are naive to the realities of life in places like Ukraine. He pointed to the international dating industry's advertising as a factor that fuels men's assumptions about their desirability abroad, saying, "It's one of their [international dating agencies] selling points. Yeah. And marketing, marketing from their employees to try to convince the guys that 20-year-old women are interested in marrying a 50-year-old American." Adam argued that Ukrainian women are generally not interested in dating men significantly older than themselves.

Adam advised that if men were interested in finding women open to large age gaps, they should consider traveling to the Philippines, which he described as an extremely poor place. "Maybe in the Philippines because they live in, you know, huts with dirt floors. But here, that's not the case. You know what I'm saying? If you're really looking for that, you shouldn't be in Ukraine; you should be going to the Philippines." Adam characterized women in the Philippines as poorer and, therefore, more desperate, making them more willing to accept larger age gaps than women in Ukraine. Beyond class differences, Adam believed that Ukrainian women are also more selective about a man's appearance and weight. He explained, "She [the office manager] was saying that the women do want a guy who's fit and in shape. They do not want to know an overweight guy, like the overweight gentleman who is like, 'Oh, I want a thin 20-year-old.' It's not going to happen. But the same in reverse; we're fit, we expect you to be fit." After years of traveling to Ukraine, Adam recognized the importance of being aware of his own sexual market value abroad and having realistic expectations for dating women in Ukraine.

Adam's biggest critique of the industry in Ukraine was the narrative that women were willing to date men significantly older than themselves. After a few visits, he realized that most Ukrainian women wanted a partner close to their own age, while many men on tour, mostly in their fifties, were searching for women under thirty-five. "A lot of the girls want a taller guy, and they do want a younger guy too. They don't want someone really old unless they're older women. Most of the older guys do not look at the older women's profiles; the most popular age is twenty-five to thirty-five, and a lot of the women over thirty-five barely get dates or are even looked at by the older guys." Adam emphasized the importance of youth in most men's search for a bride in Ukraine.

Adam further explained that dating agencies promote the fantasy of securing much younger women's labor, even if the men are older and unattractive. He said, "I think agencies make it seem like, oh, you can look any way you want, any age you want, and there's still going to be girls. They're [agencies] dealing with all these guys with these shallow expectations, and they expect the women not to have shallow expectations. They [agencies] just did a mismatch; like, oh, you can be four hundred pounds and date, you know, a supermodel type who's twenty years your junior." Based on his numerous trips to Ukraine, Adam viewed the industry with a more critical eye, particularly in terms of the narrative that any Western man can date a supermodel twenty years younger.

Adam was horrified by how some Western men arrived in Ukraine expecting women to fall at their feet, despite poor looks and hygiene. He observed, "That's what I'm saying is like, unless you want to go someplace where the woman is really, really desperate, you have to, you know, take care of yourself. Don't be showing up stinky; don't have bad breath. They [translators] were telling me some of the guys had terrible breath, that they didn't shower." Adam recognized that a man's relative affluence did not negate other factors in the sexual marketplace, like weight and appearance. The only time he thought Western men's relative affluence could outweigh being overweight or older was when women were in truly precarious economic situations. In Adam's view, women in the Philippines were in such a position, willing to accept older and unattractive men, while Ukrainian women were not.

Adam acknowledged the importance of women's aesthetic labor of beauty and how it translated into economic value in the sexual marketplace. He also recognized the value of Ukrainian women's reproductive labor and their formal work during the Communist era, saying, "So, well, and that's the thing with Eastern European women in general, is that during communism they were expected to work. They were the women workers and the mothers. So, they've been doing the whole shebang for a long f-cking time, a lot longer than American women have." For women in Ukraine, focusing solely on family could be seen as a break from the "second shift." Thus, Western men's relative affluence needed to be significant to tempt Ukrainian women into marriage and migration. Adam was not the only man I met on tour with similar observations about the sexual marketplace in Ukraine and Western men's value in that marketplace; many believed that a man's relative affluence was not enough to sustain a real relationship.

Fred had been traveling to Ukraine for years for business and would join AFA social parties while he was in town. He was even working on a guide for men to understand Ukrainian culture and dating, based on all he had learned through his travels. Much like Adam, Fred had strong opinions on Western men's value in the Ukrainian sexual marketplace. "For those who are socially awkward, just because you're in a different country doesn't mean people can't tell you're socially awkward. Do you know what I'm saying? Like, yeah, the problems that you have in the U.S.—like you're heavier set, you're socially awkward, you know, all of those kinds of things will follow you to these other countries unless they're like so poor they just do not give a f-ck about whatever." Fred criticized the assumption that being Western was enough to succeed in dating abroad unless the women were in truly precarious economic situations. He observed that men disadvantaged in their local dating markets due to personality or appearance do not always benefit by traveling to what they view as a "poorer" country. Fred also commented on the gradual decline of women's interest in the industry in Ukraine, specifically citing the quality of men traveling there in search of love: "Even the women were in general, I think, much more sincere and intrigued in the early days. I think they experienced bad experiences over that period of time. The girls found out the guys were not the cream of the crop from foreign countries, as a general statement, based on their social skills." Fred and Adam both viewed dating in economic terms, recognizing the value of their relative affluence but also acknowledging that it could only go so far in compensating for other factors of attractiveness within the dating market.

By the time we began speaking, Nikola had attended one romance tour in Ukraine and had hired two boutique matchmakers. He had already invested $20,000 into the process of traveling and hiring various dating agencies, but so far he did not consider the investment of time and money very successful, as he remained single. Beyond not finding a wife or long-term girlfriend, Nikola was frustrated that he did not receive much physical intimacy during his dates with Ukrainian women. "But I did not consider it [the tour] as a success. The reason and one of the failures is dropping this much money, going out of the country, and not being able to so much as make out with a girl, just going out on a date and then to have that third wheel [translator] there." To Nikola, the lack of physical intimacy he experienced on his tour made the experience ultimately unsuccessful, as he spent a lot of money but did not gain access to women's intimate and sexual labor. Thus, Nikola was frustrated by his lack of access to women's intimate labor in both the United States and Ukraine.

Nikola's lack of success in his search for a "hot" wife in both the United States and Ukraine further convinced him that heterosexual relationships are based on men's exchange of financial security for women's femininity capital and various forms of labor. He was largely unbothered by the prospect of marrying a woman he had little in common with, or even a woman who did not really "love" him. As a MGTOW and red pill adherent, Nikola did not believe in love. "Because love is not real, it's just a chemical emotion in our bodies, dopamine per se, a rush, but it fades away. Love is an illusion." Based on his market-based assessment of heterosexual relationships and love, Nikola's ideal wife was constructed around her aesthetic labor of hotness and the femininity capital she possessed, rather than any type of genuine love connection.

Women's Labor and Masculinity

Throughout this chapter, I illustrate how heteromasculinity is grounded in the pursuit of various forms of women's labor, including aesthetic, sexual, intimate, reproductive, and emotional, as well as the femininity capital that this labor produces. Men who join the international dating industry often feel frustrated by their inability to access these forms of labor within their local Western dating markets. Many of the men I interviewed shared experiences of loneliness, marked by failed relationships and frequent rejection. A man's lack of access to women's labor, especially aesthetic and sexual labor, diminishes his standing within the hierarchy of masculinity. Men who perceive themselves as lower in this hierarchy often engage in compensatory acts by participating in industries that commodify women's intimate labor.

Many of these men view dating in non-Western countries as a new frontier of intimacy, where they can leverage their relative affluence to enhance their sexual market value. As economic prospects for many middle- and working-class men continue to stagnate or decline in the West, some seek to reinforce their masculinity by pursuing relationships with "hot" women in countries they perceive as poorer.[38] Since masculinity is often defined by the role of economic provider, Western men facing economic challenges can still fulfill this role by seeking wives outside the West. Their participation in the international dating industry reflects the market-based logic they apply to their intimate lives.

As Rachel O'Neill observed in her study of men who pay for seduction bootcamps to learn how to access women's sexual labor, these men employ neoliberal market logic to solve their "problem" of lacking access to sex with "hot" women.[39] Paying for seduction coaching and bootcamps is just one example of the individualized and commodified solutions men adopt to gain access to women's labor, particularly that of young, thin, and blonde women. The international dating industry offers another market-based solution, providing men with opportunities to secure various forms of women's labor for more long-term and serious relationships. The men I interviewed often approached their love lives with a market-driven mindset, viewing intimate relationships through the lens of sexual market value—a concept derived from some evolutionary psychologists. While they were wary of being "scammed" or exploited for their money, they also recognized that their relative affluence in non-Western countries afforded them greater access to women's labor than they could achieve in the United States. However, most men eventually realized that their relative affluence might not be enough to secure a wife in countries like Colombia, Ukraine, or the Philippines.

3

Ukraine

The Frontier of Fantasy

Ukraine serves as a frontier of fantasy within the romance tourism and international dating industry, emerging as the most popular destination for tours, international dating sites, and boutique matchmaking agencies. A Foreign Affair (AFA) stands out by offering multicity tours across Ukraine, collaborating with local agencies in both large and small cities, including Kyiv, Mykolaiv, Kharkiv, Odesa, Poltava, and Sumy. As the most visited and popular romance tour site, Ukrainian women's femininity capital and various forms of labor are highly valued in the global dating market. This value is amplified by their whiteness and European identity, a fact explicitly acknowledged by several agency owners.

Slavic women, particularly Ukrainian, are often idealized according to white beauty standards, being characterized as tall, thin, and blonde—traits that position them as top-tier beauties within the industry. They are romanticized as model-like and seen as the ultimate trophy wife. The aesthetic labor of maintaining slim bodies and a feminine appearance through makeup and fashion generates significant femininity capital, which potential husbands can leverage to elevate their status within the male hierarchy. Many men interested in dating Ukrainian women look to Donald Trump's marriage to Melania Trump as an aspirational and achievable example within the international dating industry. The allure of exoticized white trophy wives makes Ukraine a highly profitable market, with a burgeoning cottage industry of personalized matchmakers, often local women, developing alongside the tour industry.

During the Cold War, the Eastern Bloc was portrayed as the antithesis of U.S. and Western identity. The United States depicted the Soviet Union as a bleak, gray industrial wasteland, plagued by substandard housing and inferior consumer goods. After the fall of the USSR, the region opened up to the rest of the world and quickly became synonymous with beautiful women, the sex industry, and the "mail order bride" industry, as the local economies spiraled into instability. While the international dating industry initially began in Asia, and most K-1 fiancé visas are filed in the Philippines, the fantasy of traditionally feminine white women draws the most visitors to Ukraine. Ukraine's history within the Soviet Union was initially framed as a new frontier of intimacy for Western men, offering mysterious women from behind the Iron Curtain who rejected feminism and maintained traditional gender roles.

While Ukraine served as a new frontier to find fantasy traditional white women for many of the men engaged in romance tourism, they also expressed the most distrust and fear surrounding the potential of romance "scams" in Ukraine. Many of the men I interviewed in Ukraine, and on tours in Colombia and the Philippines, argued that Ukrainian women are strategic in their affections. Most of these men held the common Western belief that intimate relationships should be separate from economic transactions, and if the two realms intermingle, it taints the notion of love.[1] In a previously published study, I argued that men's fears of scams in Ukraine are rooted in racialized assumptions about white women's greater ability to outwit them compared to women of color in the Philippines and Colombia, even though concerns about scams were expressed in all three countries.[2] However, questions of authenticity are more pronounced in Ukraine, where the U.S. Embassy in Kyiv even warns potential visitors about the prevalence of marriage and dating scams.

In addition to attributing more shrewdness and strategic thinking to Ukrainian women based on their whiteness, men tend to view them as the most aesthetically beautiful: tall, thin, and blonde. In contrast, men often describe Colombian women in a more overtly sexualized manner. The distinction men make between exoticized women as sexually appealing and white women as beautiful was noted by sociologist Ashley Mears in her study of VIP rooms in clubs.[3] Mears observed that wealthy men preferred to be surrounded by thin, white model-like women but would sexualize women of color with curvier bodies who worked as bottle service girls. Thus, the main appeal of Ukraine lies in the fantasy of accessing a white woman's aesthetic labor of beauty and femininity capital, regarded as the most desirable traits to display to other men, alongside the reproductive and intimate labor associated with a traditional marriage. Men romanticize Ukrainian women as nonfeminist white women with more traditional values than their Western counterparts, despite their fears of being scammed for a green card or money.

Scam or Bad Date?

On the first night of the romance tour in Kyiv, I dressed up in high heels and a dress for the social party at a nightclub called Sorry Babushka.[4] As I entered, I was surprised by the number of men who had shown up—over fifty, compared to the fifteen I saw in Colombia and the twenty in the Philippines. However, it quickly became apparent that there were far fewer women. I overheard several men grumbling that there were barely a hundred women in the club. With the music pumping loudly, men grabbed bottles of champagne to introduce themselves to the women. Some looked unsure of how to approach the various groups and anxiously clung to the walls.

As the night progressed, AFA held competitions on stage with prizes to encourage the women to stay until the end of the event. I was chatting with two local women when a man from the tour came over to introduce himself. Alejandro, from Mexico, had joined the tour because, in his words, "Ukrainian women are the Latin women of Eastern Europe." As the social event wound down, he became interested in Lena, a young, slender brunette dressed in a short red bodycon dress. He invited Lena, her friend Olga, and me to a nearby nightclub to keep the party going and have a "date" with Lena. We initially sat outdoors for a bite to eat, and Alejandro explained that his interest in Ukrainian women began online. He viewed them as "passionate, spicy," and as embracing traditional gender roles. However, his admiration for Lena's passion started to fade as she grew increasingly drunk and began to ignore him. Lena started dancing with a local Ukrainian man, and as she became more intoxicated, the dancing grew more intimate.

Obviously disappointed with how his "date" was turning out, Alejandro paid for all of our drinks and began to prepare to leave the nightclub. Despite his clear disappointment, he remained hopeful that the tour would still provide opportunities to meet other attractive women. Many men I interviewed on the tour would consider Lena and her friend to be "scammers," a common perception in Ukraine. Several men commented that Ukrainian women were only interested in taking advantage of foreign men on these romance tours, using them to visit fancy nightclubs and restaurants without any real interest in dating. Despite this fear of being scammed, men continue to flock to Ukraine in search of love and marriage. Their fear stems from the perception that they are unable to access Ukrainian women's intimate, emotional, and aesthetic labor, even with the significant financial investments they are willing to make.

Ukraine: Fantasies, Scams, and Whiteness

As the most popular romance tour destination for AFA and the broader industry, Ukraine stands as a frontier of fantasy and is often at the cutting edge of the international dating scene. As one of the few European locations within the industry, Ukraine's allure lies in its exoticized white women, who are still perceived as willing to perform the aesthetic labor of beauty and traditional domestic roles. This perception draws a large number of men to the industry. During AFA introductory seminars across the United States (in places like Fort

Lauderdale, Florida; Baltimore, Maryland; and Dallas, Texas), most men expressed a strong desire to visit Ukraine, idealizing Ukrainian women as the most beautiful in the world. They often described these women as tall, thin, blonde, and ultrafeminine in their attire. While in Ukraine, I learned of a common saying shared with young women that demonstrates the importance of women's aesthetic labor in Ukrainian culture: "Make sure to look your best, wherever you go, even to the grocery store, because you never know where you may meet your future husband." In contrast, I dressed as plainly as possible while in the field to avoid attracting too much attention from the men on tours. However, Ukrainian translators working for AFA would often tease me for not getting more glammed up on days when I was not attending any special events.

The consistent discourse surrounding the beauty of Ukrainian women, which men reiterated throughout my interviews, positioned Ukraine as the ultimate frontier of fantasies. Early racial theories of whiteness differentiated Eastern Europeans and Russians as "other," exoticizing them compared to Western Europeans.[5] Vladimir Putin has embraced this notion of Russia and the East as upholders of traditional gender values, opposing what he sees as the "Westernization" associated with the increasing visibility of queer people.[6] Men interested in the industry often project these political maneuvers onto the entire region, viewing Ukraine as part of a pre-feminist European East.

Despite the fantasies of Western men who envision perfect, pre-feminist, hot, thin, young blonde women eager to escape their country, many Ukrainian women are too cultured and sophisticated to be interested in these men. Most women in Odesa and Kyiv prefer to remain in major cities and are often unprepared for the rural life that awaits them in the United States outside of metropolitan areas. As mentioned in chapter 1, John Adams, the owner of AFA, explained that the 1990s were the easiest time to find potential wives for his clients, as the economic turmoil of that era made women eager to leave both Russia and Ukraine. However, as the economic situation in Ukraine has improved and stabilized, fewer women are invested in leaving the country, especially through marriage to a Western man. As a result, Ukraine largely remains a frontier of fantasy, and men are often disappointed by their lack of access to Ukrainian women's intimate and emotional labor. When these fantasies fail to materialize, men become angry and frustrated, accusing the women of being "scam artists" and gold diggers who are only after money and expensive dinners.[7] These narratives of scams and gold diggers are examples of systemic misogyny in practice; when women deny men access to their labor and femininity capital, men retaliate by labeling them as gold diggers.

Tours: Fantasies of Desirability

As John noted in the first chapter, early romance tours in Russia and Ukraine led to many success stories, with high engagement and marriage rates in the

1990s. These tales of success continue to shape men's perceptions of the industry, fueling fantasies about the accessibility of exoticized white women's aesthetic and intimate labor. Since Ukraine is the most popular tour site, AFA has developed a unique approach to its tours there. Unlike those in Colombia and the Philippines, Ukrainian tours often include multiple cities, additional social events, and a more casual format compared to the speed dating structure used at other locations.

The Ukrainian tour began with a crowded social party in Kyiv at a nightclub, a notable departure from the introductory environments in other countries. For many men on tour who are shy or socially awkward, the nightclub setting felt too similar to dating experiences in their home countries. AFA provided the men with bottles of champagne to help them introduce themselves to women. Additionally, AFA offered prizes and giveaways to women who stayed until the end of the night as an incentive to keep them engaged. However, with fifty men and only seventy-five women at the first social event, many men were disappointed. The close gender ratio made it harder for them to connect with women, which affected their feelings of desirability. The gender imbalance, which generally appeals to men on these tours, became a source of frustration in this case. The social parties lasted until eleven at night, and I joined Alejandro, Lena, and Olga at the first event in Kyiv. Other men also invited women to join them at nightclubs after the social party ended. Saturday was free for the men to date any women they liked in Kyiv before the bus departed early Sunday morning for the next city on the tour, Poltava.

Bright and early on Sunday morning, the group met outside the hotel for a four-hour bus ride from Kyiv to Poltava, a smaller city in central Ukraine. During the ride, several men, including Alec, a fifty-six-year-old eye doctor, expressed frustration about the previous night. "I didn't like the social at the nightclub," Alec said. "It was too hard to talk, too dark. It wasn't a good atmosphere. I didn't meet anyone. The women in their thirties that I wanted to meet weren't there. It was mostly women in their twenties." For Alec, the social event was disappointing due to the difficulty of communication and the age of the women attending. As we chatted on the bus, Paul, a young man in his early thirties, joined the conversation.

Paul agreed with Alec that the nightclub environment made it hard to communicate with women. "I didn't like the bar's layout," Paul said. "It wasn't conducive to talking. In tour videos from other cities, the setup seemed better for encouraging conversations. You might see three or four women sitting together, but if you only want to talk to one of them, it's hard to approach. There were no chairs to sit by anyone." Paul explained that the nightclub's layout made it more challenging to approach women comfortably. "It was harder to approach people just because of the layout," he said. "I didn't have any issues with the women themselves; they were nice. A couple of them were drunk and invited me over to their table after twenty minutes. For the most part, every woman I talked to was responsive. I had heard that women were more assertive on these tours, but they aren't at all." While Paul did not find Ukrainian women as assertive as he expected, he still considered them more assertive than American women. "Maybe they're more assertive than U.S. women, but maybe not," he said. "I do get asked to dance a lot, which is an easier way to communicate than just being in a bar." Overall, Paul felt that the social event did not offer much opportunity for deep communication. "I'm not sure if the social is the best way to meet someone," he said. "I don't know how serious the women attending are. Yesterday, I had a date with someone who said she wouldn't go to the social because it's not a place for someone who is serious." For many men on the tour, including Paul, the women who just wanted to party and drink at the nightclub did not seem ready for a serious relationship. These men often labeled younger women who were not willing to engage in the intimate and reproductive labor of courtship as "scammers."

Even though Paul did not particularly like the first social party's structure in Kyiv, he did manage to connect with a couple of women. However, he remained unconvinced that all the women attending the socials were serious about finding a relationship. "I think I'd probably come back with AFA, but you never know," he said. "I thought the arranged individual introductions were of higher quality compared to just walking up to people at a party. Are the women there to be serious? I'm not saying it was bad; I did meet someone I like from the social." To Paul, the socials were time-consuming and required a lot of effort to approach and introduce himself to women, whereas a more formalized introduction arranged by the dating agency seemed more efficient. "I think the time I spent at the social could have been better spent elsewhere," he said. "There's only so much time to spend here. How many times a year can I come back? So, I want to make the most of that time. The social is good for exposure, but I'm not sure." Paul's comments foreshadow the growing popularity of matchmaking and personalized introduction services in Ukraine and the broader industry since 2012. Most men attending socials in Ukraine wanted more assistance with formalized introductions to women, highlighting the importance of the local women staff members' labor in men's quests for love and marriage. Once we arrived in Poltava, the next city on the tour, the men went to their hotel rooms to prepare for that night's social party.

The social event in Poltava was held in a hotel's conference space, where AFA hired local DJs to provide music and entertainment, avoiding another nightclub venue. The men on tour were much happier with the larger number of women attending the Poltava event and appreciated the greater age diversity. Although the event still had an informal party atmosphere, the men had more opportunities to introduce themselves and engage in conversations. The manager of the local office in Poltava actively encouraged the men to approach different groups of women. Like in Kyiv, games and prizes were offered to encourage the women to stay throughout the evening. Despite it being a Sunday night, men were again encouraged to invite women to local bars and restaurants after the social event ended at 11 P.M. The following day, Monday, the men had time to go on dates with local women in Poltava before the bus departed early Tuesday morning for the final tour city, Sumy. In the evening, I spent time in the hotel bar with several men to hear about their experiences in Poltava.

Alec was pleased with the social party in Poltava, particularly because the women were more diverse in age. "Last night was great," he said. "So much better than Kyiv, with plenty of women in their thirties. That's really the age group I'm interested in dating." Alec had met a woman he was very interested in getting to know better and decided to stay in Poltava for a few extra days instead of continuing to Sumy. Although AFA encourages men to visit all the tour stops and meet as many women as possible to avoid disappointment if things do not work out with one woman, Alec chose to invest more time in Poltava. Having previously been on romance tours in Ukraine, he knew that the women in Sumy tended to be younger and preferred to spend his limited time with an age-appropriate woman.

In each city on the tour, men like Alec opted to stay behind to cultivate relationships with women they were particularly interested in. Those who stayed behind in Poltava had to cover their own accommodations and transportation back to Kyiv, as AFA only covers the costs for those who stay with the tour. Early Tuesday morning, the remaining men boarded a bus for another four-hour ride to Sumy, a small city near the Russian border. Upon arrival, the hotel accommodations in Sumy were not as ideal as many had hoped, as the group was split between two hotels. Sam, a thirty-eight-year-old cowboy from rural Texas, complained that his room in the overflow hotel was small and uncomfortable. Nearly half of the men were placed in the lower-quality hotel, and many expressed dissatisfaction with the accommodations, feeling they were not worth the cost of the tour. Despite their complaints, the men prepared for the final social party, which was their last chance to feel desirable among a group of younger, attractive women.

Similar to Poltava, the social party was held in a local event venue with a bar downstairs where the men frequently purchased beers. The running joke of the night was that buying beer was cheaper than bottled water, which encouraged the men to drink more. A large group of women attended, and a DJ, much like in Poltava, directed the evening's events, which included games and prizes for the women. Champagne was provided at all three locations to help the men initiate conversations with women, but most preferred beer over champagne. Several men commented that they felt most desired in Sumy, believing that the most genuine women were found in smaller, more rural cities. Sam shared his thoughts with me: "Girls in Kyiv are used to attention from foreign guys, and it takes a lot more money to impress them. Girls here in Sumy or in other small towns want to work hard to please their man and raise a family. They're way less materialistic and less likely to scam you." Men like Sam felt more desired in smaller Ukrainian cities like Sumy and Poltava compared to Kyiv, where they believed women had more exposure to foreign men, diminishing the appeal of foreign suitors.

The next day in Sumy was the final day before the group boarded the bus for another four-hour ride back to Kyiv, giving the men the least amount of time in Sumy to develop deep relationships. Sam was frustrated by the quick pace of the tour, feeling he did not have enough time to form serious connections. While Sam, as one of the younger and more conventionally attractive men on the tour, felt highly desired, he did not consider the tour successful in meeting any women for a serious relationship after it ended. Sam and the men staying in the overflow hotel were eager to get back on the bus early Friday morning, looking forward to returning to the nicer hotel in Kyiv before heading home.

Some men opted to stay longer after the tour, hoping to continue dating and building new relationships with women. When we returned to Kyiv, the big news was that Randy, a sixty-five-year-old American man, had become engaged to a thin, very attractive forty-nine-year-old local Ukrainian woman. I congratulated him in the lobby of the Kyiv hotel, and he excitedly told me he was in love and ready to get married immediately. Although many of the other men on the tour thought Randy was moving too quickly with the engagement, he knew he wanted a woman over forty who was ready to settle down. Unlike some of the men on tour who sought the attention of much younger women, Randy focused on finding an age-appropriate woman he believed genuinely desired him. "You know, a lot of these guys go for the hot young things, but I just want a woman who loves me for me—not my money or the opportunity to leave Ukraine. And I found her. And she looks better than American women ten to fifteen years younger than her." Randy's comment highlights the inherent tension in the international dating industry: men want to use their relative affluence to access women's various forms of labor and femininity capital but do not want that affluence to be the only reason they are considered desirable marriage candidates.

Labor Denied: Scams and Gold Diggers

Kyle, a teacher I met during a tour in Colombia, was one of the few men who found Ukrainian women attractive but avoided touring the country. He explained, "Ukrainian women are very athletic and disciplined, which I admire as a coach and from an athletic standpoint. But the ones I've met, at least in the United States, seemed to approach every interaction like a chess match—they were always one step ahead." Because of this, Kyle preferred Colombian women, whom he believed were more sincere in their search for a foreign husband.

Other men on the Ukraine tour discussed the dating scene as a minefield filled with potential scams and inauthentic relationships. They explained that local women are very aware of their own femininity capital as world-renowned beautiful women.[8] Timmy and Jim, whom I also met on the Colombia tour, had first encountered each other on an AFA tour in Ukraine. Since then, they had started attending tours together as travel buddies. Both white men in their early fifties with professional jobs, Timmy and Jim found it challenging to meet sincere women in Ukraine. Timmy said, "Women here know they have options. Every day, 24 hours a day, planes land, and guys keep getting dropped off— American, Italian, German, Arabian—you name it." They argued that Ukrainian women often date American men for free meals, gifts, taxis, and monetary gain.

Timmy shared that even going out to dinner in Ukraine felt like a scam. "We go to a nice restaurant, and it must have cost 90 bucks American, when you can have a nice meal for 20 bucks if you know the right places. Somehow, every girl has these discount cards. You ask for the check, and the waiter always looks at the girl, like, 'Do you have a card?'" His friend Jim quickly added, "Believe me, the discount isn't for you! They get credits." Timmy agreed, "I think they get credits for those cards. If they bring a guy from America or Germany, they don't care about spending 100 dollars. You're with a good-looking woman, and you think you have a chance—what's 100 bucks? You spend that all the time." In their view, Ukrainian women used their beauty to take advantage of foreign men willing to spend money to be in the company of beautiful women and try to access their sexual labor.

While Timmy focused on what he considered a restaurant "scam," where local women received discounts or credits for bringing foreign men to establishments, Jim highlighted what he considered a taxi "scam." "You drive around Kyiv, and it costs 12 bucks, but every time the girl asks for taxi money, it's 50 bucks." He also described how expensive every meal with a Ukrainian woman became. "The second day, I met a girl at the social, went out with her the next night, and spent a bunch of money. It was like midnight, and we were still having dinner, spending money." He then told me how he tried to spend less money the following night but was thwarted by his date.

So, the next day I was like ok, you know let's go out and I am thinking something a little more casual, I mean I was even trying to pick the restaurant based on places I had seen. So we go into this place, and she looks at the menu and she starts ordering, this, this, this, boom, boom, boom, and she closed her menu so I closed my menu and she looks at me and says, "what are you gonna have?" I am sharing with you! I'm thinking she's ordering for the both of us, the waiter and the busboy too! A ton of food! I mean this is like going to TGI Fridays and this girl still figured out how to spend 100 dollars.

Timmy laughed and jumped in exclaiming, "And they will eat every f-cking bite of it!" Despite wanting to be seen as financially generous providers, men did not want to feel "used" for expensive meals by the women they dated. They viewed their financial investments in dinners, nightclubs, and taxi rides as necessary costs in trying to access women's intimate and aesthetic labor.

Because of concerns over the authenticity of potential international relationships, men consistently consulted one another, agency employees, and website forums to gauge the trustworthiness of the women they dated on tour, especially in Ukraine. Alec, the eye doctor I met on the bus, was on his second tour to Ukraine. He told me that everyone's first tour in Ukraine was a learning curve about potential scams. "On my first tour, it took time to understand how women could scam you. You have to learn and avoid them. It's usually girls in their twenties who just want to drink, have you buy dinner and drinks, and then never see you again. So, you have to learn about that." This "learning curve" encouraged many men to attend multiple tours and become repeat clients.

I met Fred at a café, where he overheard me speaking English. When I explained my research project, he got excited. Fred was writing a guidebook for men seeking Ukrainian women and was eager to share his thoughts on the industry, as he had been traveling to Ukraine for over a decade. He documented the changes in the industry from 2005, as the industry expanded in Ukraine: "I think in the early days there was a lot of innocence and gentlemanliness on both sides. It was typically guys, maybe without social skills, maybe got divorced or even older guys may be in their 50s, 60s and even the women were . . . it is, in general, I think much more sincere." However, as the industry shifted from Russia increasingly toward Ukraine, Fred noticed a major change in the sincerity of the men and women participating: "From 2006–2008, I think people started realizing from both sides that they could benefit in other ways from it [the industry]."

As the industry continued to grow, translation services changed, which Fred argued created more of an opportunity for correspondence "scams": "For multiple reasons depending on the agency, in some cases, I think the fact that they got them so many letters that they started to automate the letters. Many girls now have a standard letter that goes back to everyone. So there is no customization. In reality some agencies of girls don't even see the letters and don't even know that you have been in contact with them." He explained to me, "Guys have spent thousands of dollars falling in love. I have heard of a guy who was crazy and came in here with a diamond ring, proposed to a girl he fell in love with by sending letters to for about four months only to find out when they first met the girl, she had not even seen the letters and they don't know who this guy is. I heard this story on a regular basis." During my own time on the tour, I heard one or two men complain that the women they conducted correspondence relationships with online would not meet them in person, but the majority of complaints men had about scams on tours concerned women using them for "free things," like expensive dinners and drinks.

Caleb, the owner of an affiliate marketing site, explained to me why Ukraine seemed to draw the largest number of men: "Well the women look good here [in Ukraine]. They really know how to take care of themselves." Beyond Ukrainian women's aesthetic labor of maintaining a beautiful appearance, Caleb explained to me that men felt more comfortable in foreign dating venues, since they had increased value and choice in women.

> Well, I mean, I think it's a challenge. First of all, if you just go into a bar, you never know. There are obviously the local websites, the Tinders and the Match.coms and that gives you some idea of someone's willingness to get involved in a new relationship and everything. But I think for many guys here who get involved in this [international dating industry], there's a certain generosity that they get in the beginning of the relationship that they do feel sort of in demand. They feel forgiven, understood. They're not questioned as much and mostly that helps them relax.

While Caleb argued that dating women in Ukraine for most of the men on tour was easier than finding a date in their local dating markets, he thought that men's chances of finding a serious relationship and increased choices was more likely in the Philippines versus Ukraine.

Caleb based this observation on the fact that women in the Philippines typically lived a more precarious lifestyle, characterized by harsher conditions, than most Ukrainian women, especially women living in cities. He argued that dating for "geeky" men is easiest in the Philippines, based on the level of poverty that many women face and the lack of college education available to many. "The biggest thing is in the Philippines, if you have a pulse, you can basically find a pretty girl who will stick with you immediately. You know Ukrainian women are far more educated and that changes the equation. They're far less desperate." As Caleb further elaborated, attending tours in the Philippines proved to be much less stressful for many of the men in comparison to Ukraine: "The Philippines, to me, the bar is so low in terms of stress and performance anxiety. It's nonexistent." In contrast, the stress of dating Ukrainian women was much higher, with men on tours consistently discussing scams.

In reality, most Ukrainian women are not scammers, and many people I interviewed emphasized that this assumption is inaccurate. Barry, who has forayed his tour participant experiences into a blog and contractual work for the agency, argues scams on tours only happen when men are acting foolish: "Scammers? It can't happen, unless you're a fool. Are they going to pick your pocket? No. If it happens, and I have seen it VERY rarely, it is because the client permitted it—a fancy meal, expensive gifts, etc." Barry also noted that many men complain about scams when they have unrealistic expectations, such as dating women much younger than themselves or sending money to women they have never met in person. He explained that men spend exorbitant amounts of money to impress women in what they consider less developed countries, and then complain about getting scammed instead of recognizing their use of financial power to advance within the intimate realm.

Ilona, a twenty-four-year-old translator with a profile on the agency website, told me that she always agrees to dates with men visiting Ukraine to prove that she is in fact a real woman, and not a scammer. She explained to me, "I can meet people, because if I refuse to meet I know clearly that if I refuse to meet some guy, who wants to meet me via some marriage . . . dating service, he's . . . he will probably, 90% or 80% he will write to the site or write on the service that I'm a scam girl." Ilona believed that many men called Ukrainian women scammers based on their own unrealistic dating expectations: "Many [men] it seems like if they have bad luck, they start to complain that all the girls are scammers, that this is shit f-cking Ukraine." Although Ilona was not interested in seriously dating or marrying most of the men she met from the site, she still wanted to meet them for at least one date. Despite men's fears of being "scammed" for meals, money, or a green card, they continued to flock to Ukraine in search of exoticized white women, making it the most popular tour location until the outbreak of full-scale war with Russia in February 2022.

White Women Performing Traditional Labor

While many marriage migrants are from Asia and Latin America, the image most commonly associated with the "mail order bride" is the Russian bride, largely due to their whiteness.[9] Nicole Constable found that after the fall of the Soviet Union, women from the former Soviet bloc surpassed Filipinas in the romance tour industry, as they were often touted as a "superior" choice based on their whiteness.[10] Ingrid Piller claims that Russian women's main competitive edge is their race: they are exoticized yet still considered "white."[11] Sonja Luehrmann noted that women in Russia seem to offer all the traditional values men used to look to Asia for but fit more neatly into the racial hierarchies of the United States and may be less recognized as "mail order brides" when appearing with their husbands in public, echoing John Adams's understanding for the popularity of Ukrainian brides.[12] Ukrainian women are often considered top candidates for American men searching for brides, valued for both their traditional values and sexuality.[13]

Buck, the tour leader from AFA assigned to the Ukraine tour, was a former successful client who worked for AFA for years. Although he moved to Phoenix for work, his wife and children remained in the Midwest. Buck wrote a guidebook for AFA clients offering advice about the industry, but the book primarily focused on women from the former Soviet region. While Buck mentioned that Ukraine was the most popular tour site, he noted that the Philippines was rapidly growing in popularity. He also differentiated between the goals of men attending tours in the Philippines and those attending tours in Ukraine. "Most of the men who are going to the Philippines want to meet somebody who is ok with the broad age realms, somebody who they view as not university-educated, with very, very traditional marriage and family values. People who come to Ukraine, I think, they expect university-educated women who are professional, obviously very intelligent—not that the women in anywhere else aren't—but sophisticated, and sophistication is important to some men—to have a conversation. Your average CEO or corporate vice presidents." He explained to me that whiteness and a European identity are often linked in men's minds to a level of sophistication and a class identity that they often do not necessarily apply to women in Asia and Latin America.

> It's gonna get hard to go to the Philippines and find somebody who can really have a, you know, good conversation on this level, when it comes to accounting and math, those kinds of things. So, I think guys are looking for themselves. So, I think most of the guys who are going to the Philippines are probably not university-educated, white-collar professionals. In Latin America, I think typically you'll see what you see in the Philippines, I think most of the guys who go to Latin America are going to be blue-collar guys.

Thus, Buck distinguishes between women from Ukraine and those from other tour locations, as well as between the men who attend the tours. This distinction is based on the racialized notion that Ukrainian women are more educated and sophisticated, while women from Latin America and Asia are perceived as less educated and less capable of engaging in conversations with CEOs.

When I asked Brian, the brother of one of the AFA owners who married a Filipina woman, why Ukraine is the most popular site, he frankly replied, "Without sounding racist: they're white. So, you're not going to get as many people to come here [the Philippines], even though the girls are beautiful and probably just as loving and caring and maybe even more so, as far as family oriented. Still, it's just a niche market. Same with China. Same with Latin America." This acknowledgment from AFA's leadership highlights the role of race in determining the main international dating market versus niche markets in more racially "exotic" locations. The industry saw significant expansion after the fall of the USSR in the early 1990s, shifting much of its infrastructure from Asia to Eastern Europe.

When I asked John, the public-facing owner of AFA, about why men prefer Ukrainian women over others, he pointed out that the dynamic is different when both parties in a relationship are the same race. This makes the origin of the relationship less obvious. He explained, "It's [interracial dating] not the dynamic in, uh, the Ukraine, in Eastern Europe because everyone's Caucasian. Right. And there's the opposite of that is, that some men would rather not go to the

Philippines because it's such a, it's just a statement. It's pronounced that, oh, you went to the Philippines, and you got married and some men are afraid of that stigma." To many men in the industry, marrying an Asian or Latin American woman signaled that the couple met through the industry, which is still stigmatized in the general public.

Alec, the eye doctor I interviewed, traced his interest in Ukrainian women to his heritage as well as their stereotypically "white" appearance. "My grandparents are from Ukraine. So that was one of the main reasons. I mean countries around the world that AFA goes, like the Philippines, South America. I wasn't interested in going there. I am not attracted to those women. I am more into the Slavic and Swedish look. Very fair, light eyes, light hair." Like Alec, Paul from the bus ride interview also traced his interest in dating Ukrainian women back to his heritage, as his grandparents had immigrated to the United States from Ukraine. Paul even learned basic Russian in preparation for his trip and was privy to conversations women and employees had about him, both negative and positive. Paul also defined his ideal woman in terms of a stereotypically white appearance.

Brad, a repeat tour client and part-time AFA employee, described his interest in Ukrainian women as based on their resemblance to June Cleaver and her traditional forms of reproductive and aesthetic labor. He explained,

> I mean, it's just, they [Ukrainian women] have this blonde, blue eyed—they dress to kill, and they're just so ladylike. I tell you what, it's a lot like dating June Cleaver from *Leave It to Beaver*. I can see them wearing pearls making borscht with an apron in the kitchen. They really value that. Funny thing. You know, you'd walk to a restaurant, and you order borscht. "Oh, this is really good," and then every woman I ever went out with, she goes, "I make it better." Every time! You gotta love it!

Most men did not explicitly identify race as the motivating factor for attending a tour in Ukraine. Instead, they framed their interest in Ukrainian women over Latin or Asian women in terms of personal taste and preference, a pattern sociologists studying racial preferences in online dating have also observed.[14] When I asked Brad, "What do you think draws most of these men to Ukraine over other tour locations?" Brad answered, "The women! I think that if you've [the researcher] already been to Latin America, it has to be your taste. Or if you're into Asian women, it has to be your taste. You're going to the Philippines. You'll see." Many AFA employees also linked racialized desirabilities to questions of personal taste and preference.

Even men of color fantasized about accessing white women's aesthetic labor. I met numerous Latino men, beyond Alejandro, interested in marrying Ukrainian women, and sometimes Ukrainian women only. Nikola, from the introduction, described the racialized appearance of Ukrainian women as his beauty ideal.

Despite his young age, Nikola was dissatisfied with the dating scene in Los Angeles and the decline of traditional family values in U.S. society. He believes that the answer to his dating woes lies in the former Soviet Union, where Slavic culture encourages women to embrace traditional family values and healthier lifestyles. Nikola defines traditional family values as women staying home to raise children and, more importantly, putting their husband first, demonstrating selflessness in their emotional labor.

While Nikola describes his ideal woman in terms of traditional values, he is more interested in finding a "hot blonde, thin Slavic" woman who would often be "out of his league" in the Los Angeles dating market. He believes that his status as an American, despite his Mexican heritage, will increase his sexual market value in Ukraine. Nikola explained that he wants an attractive wife to impress other men and appear more intelligent and successful: "Guys want the hottest girls possible so that we can pass the best genes on to our kids. That's why I like Slavic girls. They have that thin body type, feminine appearance, and traditional values. Having a hot girl like that lets other guys know you are successful and smart. I mean, there's a study that shows rich CEOs with higher IQs are attracted to slim, hot girls."

Nikola views intimacy as a market-based exchange, feeling that he needs to accumulate wealth before gaining access to women with high femininity capital he deems "hot" enough. He concluded, "If I fail again this year, I might not bother dating until I'm older and have more money . . . Seems like if I want the hot model type, I need the money to back her . . . but that's what I'm after . . . so I'd rather wait a few years and go back." Ultimately, Nikola prioritizes women's aesthetic labor—beauty and femininity capital—over other considerations, such as reproductive labor, and is willing to trade his future financial security for the chance to have a "hot" wife.

Extracting Employees' Labor

After joining the tour in Ukraine, it became clear that the Arizona AFA office plays a much more active role in the romance tour process than other locations. The tour was led by two employees from the Phoenix AFA office, Alina and Buck, along with Brad, a volunteer leader who had previously appeared on a television special with AFA. Alina, a Russian woman who married an American and later moved to Phoenix after their separation, has worked for AFA for several years and often leads tours in Ukraine. I recognized Brad immediately upon entering the hotel lobby where the men were staying. He had been featured in a *Nightline* episode about AFA and the "mail order bride" industry in Ukraine, which my mother had sent me to help with my research project. I was surprised to see him in Kyiv, but he was there to help run the tour and complete filming for a documentary he was involved in, titled *Love Me*. Although Brad was volunteering, not working as an employee, he was excited to assist with the tour, as it was his eleventh time visiting Ukraine. He had developed many friendships across the country and was particularly enthusiastic about the tour's second stop in Poltava, his favorite city. "Oh, I have so many friends there! You will see; I am even friends with the DJs who play at the social. They are a bunch of fun young Ukrainian guys," he exclaimed. Even in his late sixties, Brad was eager to keep the party going throughout the tour.

All the local translators on the tours in Ukraine were women, and they were assigned to men during social events to facilitate communication. These translators had mixed opinions about the men on the tour, as many were also listed as profiles on the website. On the night of the first social event, I approached the nightclub, unsure if I was in the right place. I noticed a few young women outside smoking cigarettes and asked if they were there for the event. They nodded, and I began talking with Lena, a woman working as a translator for the evening. She was mentally preparing herself for the chaos of the nightclub, following her assigned client for the night. Lena, engaged to a man from Oregon whom she met during a romance tour in Kyiv six months earlier, exemplified a translator who dated foreign men. Despite her engagement, she joked about being interested in one of the wealthy men on the tour and flirted with him during the party.

Throughout the tour, the men were in constant communication with the women translators and office staff to arrange dates with women in the AFA database who chose not to attend the social events. The translators and staff worked long hours to ensure the clients' happiness, providing emotional support, relationship advice, and tools to navigate cultural exchanges. By the end of the week, Lena, along with the local managers and other translators, was exhausted from being on call for the entire tour. She particularly complained about one client, Rich, who hired her to work as a translator outside of the included translations in his tour package.

Rich, a fifty-year-old heavy-set engineer from the United States, and his date, who took a train into Kyiv from a smaller town for the date, hired Lena to translate for an evening date. Lena commented on how direct the woman was in asking Rich about his financial situation: "She's really, she's beautiful. But she's stupid. She starts telling Rich, 'You know, I have a small child, small son, and if I will come to your country, you need to support me,'—MUST, even not have, MUST! The woman said, 'You must support me, because I don't know language and I'm not going to work' and he was like, 'Ok, that's not a problem, yes, I will, I'll do everything for you.'" Lena rolled her eyes while telling me this story, as she could not believe the stupid behaviors of either party on the date. When Rich's date got up to use the restroom, Lena tried to explain to him that this woman was just interested in his money: "I explained to him that she's not interested, and I explained to him that she's a terrible person. He was like, 'Ok, let it be. Tomorrow in the morning she will leave Kyiv, that's all. And now we are coming upstairs just to sleep, to rest, that's all.' So, they went upstairs, and I don't know what has happened. He didn't pay me that night." Frustrated and without payment, she went home for the night angry.

The next day, Lena tried to get the office to contact Rich for her payment. He had promised that someone was sending him money for her translation work and that he would bring the money to the local office. "Someone had to send him money, but nothing happened. He promised me he would bring this money to the office, but we don't have his phone number, like they don't have his phone number, they don't know where he stayed. So, $90 are somewhere. Probably he already left the country." Although frustrated by the wage theft, Lena was not surprised by Rich's behavior, considering him a foolish older man searching for much younger women to marry. "Cause, I don't know, he's [Rich] almost sixty, and he decided to date a young girl. Just think, she will not be interested in you. She will be interested in your money." Ultimately, Lena questioned the judgment of many men involved in the tours or email correspondence. "I've got no idea why all those old men, all those old guys, choose young ladies. Just think before you do." By the time I left Ukraine, Lena still had not received her payment from Rich.

Yekaterina, another translator in the Kyiv office, embodied the ideal standard of beauty that most men on romance tours sought: a thin, blonde woman in her early twenties with blue eyes. When I asked her about translating for dates and whether men hit on her while she worked, she replied, "Almost all the time, unfortunately! I'm young, I'm pretty. They're dating women of mostly 35, 40 years old, and . . . I have good English. Maybe that's it. Sometimes those people they even say, 'Ok, you're talking good, I'm so bored, let's go for a walk, I'm gonna pay you for translations.'" I also asked Yekaterina if men typically dated women her age. She told me she refused to work with men trying to date significantly younger women, cringing as she said, "Actually I didn't take such translations, such dates, cause I don't like that. It's weird. I can't, I can't." She commented that Western men idealized Ukrainian women for their aesthetic and reproductive labor, which explained the industry's popularity: "They know that Ukrainian women are good in house holding. They know that everybody here knows how to cook, to clean, how to take care of a man, mostly. Also, they say that Ukrainian women are taking care of themselves as well. Those huge heels, the skirts, make up, hairstyles . . . they are beautiful, attractive blah blah." Yekaterina's comments point to the importance of women's aesthetic labor of maintaining "feminine" beauty standards and the importance of their reproductive and intimate labor dedicated to caring for their men partners.

Alexandra worked for AFA as a translator and was also listed on the website as a profile open to dating men from abroad. By the time we met, Alexandra had been working in the industry for nearly a decade: "I started translating for a dating site and services in 2004. Though at that moment I already had a good experience in working with couples, I also probably had two couples which got on well together and one couple which eventually got married." Throughout her time working as a translator and dating men through AFA, Alexandra developed strong opinions about the reason men often came to Ukraine in search of a wife, considering the discourse surrounding women like herself to be a type of dating agency propaganda spread to men: "Maybe a lot of men think that women here like to cook and clean, it depends on some propaganda, American propaganda that Ukrainian girls like to cook, and they like to clean up and they all are pretty." Alexandra's quote echoes the sentiments expressed by Yekaterina that men came to Ukraine looking to extract women's aesthetic and reproductive labors based on a certain narrative surrounding Ukrainian women.

When I asked Alexandra about her impressions of the American men coming to Ukraine in search of a wife, she expressed frustration with their perception of Ukrainian women as merely housewives with no other ambitions or skills: "Some of them [American men] think that it's very easy to come to another culture, to take some girl from another country who probably doesn't speak English or who speaks a little bit of English and of course maybe she can cook or she can clean up but, excuse me, she has university degree or she is quite well off here." Alexandra's words challenge the common assumption many American men have when they first join a romance tour: that all Ukrainian women are poor and desperate for a foreign knight in shining armor to rescue them.

Alexandra was shocked and dismayed by men's lack of cultural preparation before coming to Ukraine in search of a serious relationship: "Yes, and a lot of guys think that they can come here, take a wife, this will be serious and go away [back to their home country]. No culture differences, no awareness in our culture, no awareness in anything. They don't know anything about Ukraine, they just want a beautiful wife." To some Ukrainian women like Alexandra, the men on tour did not put much effort into learning Ukrainian culture. "And in our culture, we are up brought up on books, some fairy tales about princesses from childhood and when some ugly, fat . . . American man probably 52, 53, 56 comes and says that he is eager somebody to love him just for what he is, it's just . . ." Alexandra then just sighed, demonstrating her frustration with many men's unrealistic expectations for wanting the hottest and youngest woman possible.

Alexandra also shared her experiences with men who complained when her translating services seemed too expensive: "A lot of men complain, when I interpret, a lot of men complain about expensive services of the interpreter. When they come here and you tell them that it's 20 dollars per hour, their eyes are like that big and they say, 'That's very, very expensive. That's f-cking expensive,' and what should I say? I don't know what . . ." In Alexandra's role as both a translator and profile on the site, she was keenly aware of how men often portrayed Ukrainian women as "scammers" if they were denied access to women's intimate labor.

Even though Alexandra was interested in potentially marrying a man from abroad, she did not want to be simply a housewife with no type of financial independence: "I don't need to be married and I don't need to be a housewife. Of course, probably, if I fell in love, I would get married and I would probably be a housewife for some time in some other country. But if I'm a housewife, I want to get what I can get for myself. All the cosmetics, all these shoes." For this reason, Alexandra identified as an independent woman: "So, I'm independent in this way and I'm not looking for someone just to get me these things or for that reason." She told me about how she had broken up with a German man who only wanted her to stay in the house to cook and clean for him: "That guy just didn't want to support me. He even didn't want me to pass the German courses, I didn't have that much practice and I needed to pass the German courses in Germany and for me to get work if I get married with him. And he told me that my German was all right and we could practice it in the kitchen." Thus, the one relationship she had seriously pursued with a foreign man ended when he did not want to let her maintain a semi-independent life.

Conclusion

Ukraine serves as the frontier for men's fantasies of traditional, thin white women whose labor is still accessible. The international dating industry often links Ukrainian women's whiteness with the traditional values once attributed to white middle-class American women of the 1950s. These women are expected to perform aesthetic labor by remaining thin and beautiful, maintain their femininity capital, and engage in reproductive labor by caring for husbands, children, and the home. Additionally, they provide intimate labor, offering sex and emotional support. Since the 1990s, after the dissolution of the Soviet Union, Ukraine has surpassed the Philippines in popularity as a destination for international marriage. Employees of AFA acknowledge that Ukraine's appeal as a tour destination is based on women's association with whiteness. As John pointed out, many men feel that the origins of their relationships are more "hidden" with white women compared to women from Asia or Latin America.

However, the constant influx of foreign men looking for women to have intimate relationships with provide Ukrainian women with increased choices. Less women were choosing to participate in the industry as time went on, especially younger women, who often wanted to meet and marry Ukrainian men. However, the constant influx of foreign men seeking relationships with Ukrainian women has provided these women with more choices. Some men label Ukrainian women as "scammers" when they do not get the expected outcomes. They might complain about taking women to expensive meals only to be ignored afterward, or about paying for taxi rides home, suspecting the women of pocketing the money or charging extra. When men feel they have been denied women's intimate or sexual labor, despite their financial investment in the industry, they "punish" women by accusing them of scamming or attempt to have them removed from dating websites.

The ongoing war in Ukraine is significantly altering the international dating industry, as Ukraine was the top destination for many companies. For instance, Mark Davis shut down Dream Connections tours, stating that the war has made it impossible to continue their tour-based business, which lacked a correspondence component. Many boutique matchmakers are now trying to operate abroad, matching Ukrainian refugees with local men in countries like Germany and Bulgaria. Group romance tours have been indefinitely paused due to the dangerous travel conditions, though some men still travel to Ukraine alone to meet women in person. Meanwhile, online correspondence has increased, with many men seeing the war as an opportunity to use their safety and relative wealth to find a Ukrainian girlfriend or wife. The conclusion will explore the war's impact on the industry in greater depth.

4

Colombia

The Sexualized Frontier

In the contemporary international dating industry, Colombia is seen as a destination for sex, fun, and danger, attracting Western men who seek to exploit the sexual and aesthetic labor of local women. The image of sexy, curvy, and "spicy" Latina women dominates men's imaginations, drawing them to Colombia in search of love. Many men view Colombian women as hyperfeminine and hypersexual, with some engaging in the sex tourism industry while pursuing romantic connections. These expectations of women's sexy appearance, particularly in terms of dress, further fuel perceptions of their supposed sexual prowess. The discourse around Colombian women builds on centuries of colonial narratives that hypersexualize and racialize women in colonized regions, framing them as sources of labor to be extracted.[1] Colombian women's femininity is often tied to their sexual and aesthetic labor, with a particular emphasis on their sexual labor.

Throughout the tour experience, men extracted intimate and aesthetic forms of labor from the women they dated, as well as from those they encountered in sex work clubs and those working for the agency as translators and managers. Colombian women provided sexual, intimate, and emotional labor to men through dates and participation in the sex tourism industry, which often boosted the men's sense of masculinity and self-esteem compared to their experiences in their home countries. Men who felt overlooked or undervalued in their local dating markets often cited an increase in their attractiveness in Colombia, largely due to their relative wealth as Westerners.

An additional factor driving men's interest in Colombia is its association with danger. Many of the men I interviewed felt "cool" and "brave" for traveling to a country known for narco-trafficking, Pablo Escobar, guerrillas, and kidnappings. Friends and family often expressed concern about their travels, but the men soon realized that Medellín is a modern, clean, and up-to-date city with heavy security in the tourist zone, El Poblado. Aside from concerns about "Devil's Breath" (scopolamine), most of the men I spoke with found Medellín to be a fun and safe place to party.[2] However, many men in Medellín avoided women they considered too dark-skinned, preferring light-skinned brunettes who better fit into the American racial hierarchy.

Sex and Fun

I woke up early on the fifth day of the tour to interview Tim and Jimmy. Both men, in their mid-fifties at the time, lived in Texas. Tim, who stood five foot ten inches tall with blue eyes and a noticeable belly, always dressed in stereotypical Texan fashion—large belt buckles and flannel button-up shirts. Jimmy, also five foot ten inches tall but very thin, preferred polo shirts and khaki pants. Despite their different styles, the two became fast friends during an A Foreign Affair tour in Ukraine in early 2002. Tim loved traveling the world and meeting beautiful women, finding romance tours ideal. "I've been to Ukraine maybe three or four times," he said. "I went to Lima, Peru, once. I've been here [in Medellín] twice, and I've been to Costa Rica six times. I wasn't on a tour there, but I know they have tours. I met a girl through the agency out there." Jimmy, on the other hand, attended three tours in Ukraine and one in Colombia.

After meeting on tour in Ukraine, Tim and Jimmy decided to become tour buddies. Despite the competition among men on these tours, many developed deep friendships. A common theme that emerged in my discussions with men was the lasting nature of these friendships, often outlasting their relationships with women abroad. Like many others, Jimmy and Tim bonded and decided to continue touring together. According to Tim:

> I like to travel. I mean, I met Jimmy on the tour in Kyiv and he told me he liked to travel too. I always hated to travel alone but now all my buddies that I got don't have enough money to travel. They don't have enough money or funds, or they can't take off [from work], so that's been great meeting Jimmy, because we kind of have a lot of things in common. Even when I went to Peru by myself . . . you know it was just like you are always with a great group of guys.

As Tim and Jimmy were explaining their tour friendship to me, Derrick and Vincent joined us for the interview.

Derrick and Vincent were both younger men, in their late thirties, and Derrick was also from Texas. While Tim seemed Texan, Derrick was even more obvious in his cowboy boots and large cowboy hat. A small man with bright blue eyes and blonde hair, Derrick was one of the few working-class men I met during my time on romance tours, as he worked as a truck driver. Derrick told me that he had scrimped and saved to come on the trip to Colombia and that he wanted to find a woman who had kids, as he already had four kids by his late thirties. Vincent, also in his late thirties, was the opposite of Derrick in many ways—a tall, successful Latino marketing executive living in Los Angeles but quiet and introverted. Vincent explained that he wanted to travel to Colombia, but none of his friends were willing to join him. He figured that joining a tour would allow him to meet new people, including single women. After the interview, the five of us decided to go to the casino. Afterward, Jimmy left for one final date before his flight the next morning.

Tim invited the rest of us to have one last dinner together at a small outdoor restaurant. Over a bottle of local rum, he suggested we all go to a strip club that night. We got into a taxi and arrived at a large warehouse-like building that housed a huge strip club. Unlike strip clubs in the United States, this one in Medellín had a second floor with numerous private rooms that men could rent by the hour. The strippers danced briefly to advertise themselves to the men, and after each performance, men had the opportunity to pay for private time upstairs. As we sat down at a table, Tim bought a round of shots and leaned over to me, saying, "I'm going to get you drunk so we can hook up." I laughed and took my shot, knowing there was no chance of that happening.

Within our group, Tim was the clear life of the party and an expert on strip clubs and sex work in Colombia. As we watched the performances, one woman stood out to Vincent, and Tim waved her over. A petite, curvy brunette joined us, and Tim immediately encouraged her to sit on Vincent's lap. Although shy at first, Vincent's fluency in Spanish helped him ease into asking her to go upstairs with him. He returned half an hour later with an excited grin, and Tim proudly patted him on the back for "scoring" with his encouragement. Emboldened by Vincent's example, Derrick decided to follow suit. He waved over another petite, curvy woman with long dyed blonde hair. Vincent negotiated on Derrick's behalf, and the two disappeared upstairs.

At this point, Tim rounded up Vincent and told me they needed to catch a taxi back to the hotel to make their early morning flight. He suggested I wait for Derrick to finish upstairs and share a cab with him. While waiting for Derrick, the club closed and emptied. The performers and clientele left, and I stood by the bar as the bartenders and security guards cleaned up and counted the night's earnings. After what felt like forever, Derrick finally emerged, hand in hand with the same sex worker. He drunkenly asked if he could borrow $100 to pay the woman to accompany him back to the hotel. I laughed and told him, "Derrick, you're crazy. You know I don't have that kind of money with me. Get in the cab!" This story illustrates how common men's ventures into Colombian sex work were, even as they searched for love and marriage.

Colombia es Pasión: Women's Sexual
and Aesthetic Labor

Since 2005, Colombia has worked to rebrand itself, shifting its image from a country associated with narco-trafficking and violence to one recognized for its biodiversity and hardworking people. The international tourism and investment campaign *Colombia es Pasión* showcases Colombian women as part of the nation's natural landscape and beauty. Even the campaign's logo—a lopsided heart with a flame in the middle—resembles a curvy woman's midsection, further emphasizing this connection.[3] Feminist scholar Felicity Schaeffer argues that the Colombian state's marketing campaign utilizes the passion of its citizens' bodies to court foreign investments and to normalize heterosexual romantic exchanges across cultures.[4]

Men interested in attending romance tours in Colombia often mentioned women's sexuality and the prevalence of sex work, as sex work is legal and a common attraction to the country.[5] Certain countries are associated with sex tourism, and Colombia is on the list with places like Thailand, Brazil, Cuba, and the Dominican Republic.[6] Colombia is what Denise Brennan terms a "sexscape," which she defines as geographic spaces that are exoticized and sexualized.[7]

Colombia's Caribbean coast, particularly the city of Cartagena, has long been associated with sex tourism. Cartagena became infamous after the 2012 scandal involving at least nine American Secret Service agents and local sex workers. During President Obama's visit to the Summit of the Americas in Cartagena, the agents visited a high-end local strip club and paid $60 to bring two women back to the Hotel Caribe. The next morning, one of the sex workers demanded the $800 "gift" an agent had promised her the previous night. When a dispute arose between the agents and the women, local police were called to intervene.[8]

The themes of passion, exotic sensuality, and an element of danger heavily influence men's perceptions of Colombia and Colombian women. Many brothels operate as strip clubs, like the one I visited in Medellín, but sex work is prevalent everywhere tourists go, including nightclubs, bars, and local attractions. The widespread availability of sex work, along with easy access to street drugs like cocaine and cannabis, creates a party atmosphere laced with risk.

U.S. media portrayals of Colombian women—and Latina women in general—as sexual, curvaceous, and passionate fuel interest in Colombia's sex tourism industry, bringing vital tourism dollars into the economy. In my interviews with men on tour, the emphasis on passion, sexuality, and curvy bodies dominated discussions about Colombian women. One Cuban American man, Sal, shared his thoughts in Medellín, saying, "I knew a Calina [a woman from Cali, Colombia] in the States, and wow! They are spunky! Nice but spunky. And very sexual. Very sexual." Sal repeatedly highlighted the sexual and lively nature of

Colombian women as the main attraction that drew him to Colombia in search of romance.

Searching for Sexual and Aesthetic Labor

I met Salvatore, a sixty-five-year-old Cuban from Miami, in Medellín after his recent breakup with a younger woman in Cartagena. Despite his poor track record with much younger girlfriends, Sal continued to pursue women in their twenties. In fact, the oldest woman he was interested in was thirty. His previous girlfriend, Nidia, was in her early twenties. Salvatore admitted that Nidia was too young for him and said they were just having "fun" during his first tour. However, agency workers mentioned that he had started the paperwork to bring her to the United States. The relationship ended when Nidia's mother insisted on accompanying her daughter if she were to move to the United States. While dating Nidia, Sal told the agency staff that she was great in bed but found it odd that she refused to kiss him. The translators working on the tour shared with the agency that Sal took Nidia shopping on their first date, and she returned to his hotel with bags full of purchases.

Given that agencies emphasize Colombian women's devotion to their families, it is not surprising that many American men are drawn to Colombia in hopes of finding a woman who would "take care" of them and provide emotional support. A man I met on a tour in the Philippines, Matt, spoke about his friend's Latina wife as an example of the emotional labor women from other countries provide. He explained, "You know, a guy I work with has been married to a lady from Ecuador for 15 years. It's funny—they both spend all day every day helping each other out. Every day she gets up, cooks him breakfast, sends him off to work, and welcomes him home. She doesn't work, and I'm sure she treats him just as well as the day she met him." Matt's description focused on how this Ecuadorian woman's life revolved around supporting her husband, cooking for him, and staying home to greet him each day.

Many men view women's performance of reproductive labor as an "act of love" and as "taking care" of them.[9] Mike's travel partner, Peter, a lifelong bachelor in his early fifties, linked his interest in Colombian women to their family values and their commitment to maintaining their appearance for their husbands. Peter said:

And I did a lot of research on women and it just seemed like Colombian women is a whole world I found, I love the culture, I love the fact it's kind of Latino-European mix, not just the physical characteristics, but I love their attitude towards, they seem like . . . of course everybody's different, but they seem like . . . as a general rule, Colombian women have a very . . . values-moral-family-type familiar kinda culture, but they also seem to be like "But I wanna look nice, dress nice and be sexy, and I'll take care of my guy."

Peter's statement highlights the appeal of Colombian women's aesthetic labor and femininity, as well as their willingness to perform reproductive, intimate, and emotional labor—qualities he found lacking in women from the United States.

Similarly, Kyle also described Colombian women as desirable in terms of the labor they put into maintaining a beautiful appearance since looking feminine with makeup, hair done, and so on, requires labor: "Well, they dress like there's no tomorrow. Everyone, well . . . not everyone, but most of them are very good . . . like they put on makeup like a makeup artist would put on makeup. They never really look bad, so they rely on that, looking really great." Kyle directly pointed to the large amounts of labor that Colombian women spend on "looking good" and interpreted their labor as an example of the way they prioritize aesthetic labor in comparison to women in the United States: "People here [Colombia] are much more concerned about their appearance." Kyle compared this to women in the United States, whom he felt prioritized their careers over their appearance or intimate relationships.

Kyle believed that women in the United States worked too much and there-fore had less time for him: "Atlanta is a real business town so all the ladies there beyond their twenties are real career-oriented and they just work a lot of hours and have a lot of travel, so when they would come home they wouldn't want to go anywhere or do anything because they were tired." One of the main things Kyle wanted was a travel partner, as he was already retired from teaching and pursuing his passion of filming documentaries: "But again, I'm in a unique posi-tion since I don't have to work. Three times a year I will go somewhere and work for a month on some project. I wouldn't want someone who came to the United States and [would] have to work." Kyle would rather have a wife whose employ-ment is flexible, so she can accompany him in his travels and be his support sys-tem while he pursues his passion, demonstrating the asymmetrical support role that men expect women to be in.

While American men are looking for more "traditional" wives, they do not want the poorest of the poor women, the women who are desperate to leave a country, or the women who are simply using foreign men for their money, since men view relationships with economic motivations as insincere. Nicole Consta-ble also found that American men seek women who are not the poorest of the poor, to ensure the woman's sincerity in marrying them.[10] Kyle considered Colombian women to be of a higher social class status than women he met on tour in Costa Rica: "The main thing was that the girls, at least the ones I met at the social [in Costa Rica], none of them were really professional. The women there were kind of on welfare and had several children. Some had tattoos. I think they are mostly looking for a guy from America with a little bit of money to send them money from time to time and come to see them from time to time, but they weren't really looking for relationships or like marriage or anything."

Kyle was extremely disappointed with his tour in Costa Rica and asked John from AFA for his recommendations regarding which tour had the women most suited to his requirements: "He said, well for what you're looking for, a professional woman and attractive and in their thirties or forties, he said Medellín, Colombia is the place." He differentiated the women in Medellín from the women in Costa Rica based on their professionalism: "Well the ladies here are just . . . as far as the ladies go, they are beautiful and professional and educated. Even the ones that don't speak much English seem to have some type of job here that keeps them going whereas in Costa Rica it seemed like they just don't work there." Professional women with decent jobs within their own countries seemed to assure American men that these women were not simply after their money or citizenship, as the fear of scams was still present in Colombia but not as ubiquitous as the fear in Ukraine.

The "Dangerous" Frontier

As my experience with the strip club/brothel revealed, I quickly became aware of the overlap between sex and romance tourism in Colombia during my first romance tour. While I suspect that men in Ukraine and the Philippines engage in similar practices, the overlap in Colombia was much more overt. The country is often portrayed as a party destination, offering drugs, beaches, and beautiful women. Once largely closed off to tourism due to periods of violence, Colombia is now being "rediscovered" by men from Western countries, particularly the United States. They see it as a new type of dangerous frontier—risky, yet filled with the potential rewards of women willing to perform the aesthetic and sexual labor they desire.

The rise of what scholars term "dark" or "toxic" tourism—visits to places like Auschwitz or Chernobyl—centers on the dangers and horrors of the past.[11] Although Colombia is not associated with radioactivity or genocide, the violence linked to narco-trafficking in the 1980s and 1990s, especially kidnappings and bombings, continues to shape people's perceptions of the country. Although most of these men felt safe from such threats, they also felt brave compared to their loved ones who were too afraid to travel to Colombia.

However, AFA advises men not to stray too far from the group, as the agency cannot assist if they venture out alone. On my second romance tour in Medellín in 2016, Henry, a fifty-year-old white man dressed in cargo shorts and glasses, decided to explore the local nightlife on his own, outside of tour-sanctioned events. He ended up at a small local music club, dancing with a beautiful woman. Still in shock when he recounted the story to me, Henry described how he was drugged with "Devil's Breath" (scopolamine) and robbed.

At the club, Henry recalled the woman he was dancing with kept rubbing on his arm, which is a common way that Devil's Breath is transmitted to potential victims (at times, people will blow it in someone's face). He began to feel strange as the woman he danced with led him out of the club, and he described the feeling as "like being drunk, but aware. Like I couldn't really move my body well, but I knew what was going on. She took me to an ATM and made me pull out a bunch of money and she just left me there. I knew I didn't want her to take my money, but I couldn't do anything to stop her." Henry woke up the next morning underneath the ATM in a grocery store when a grocery store clerk woke him up to open the store.

Despite this experience, Henry did not consider Colombia dangerous. He recognized that venturing off on his own was not the best decision. International dating agencies organize activities and assist men with their dates and outings to help avoid dangerous situations, as many of their clients are inexperienced travelers. However, the element of risk in Colombia adds to the thrill of pursuing love, sex, and intimacy. As many men told me, intimate relationships can be risky, even in the United States.

Mike and Peter, longtime friends from Boca Raton, Florida, were both in their late fifties, white, upper-middle-class businessmen when I met them on tour in Colombia. They felt overlooked and taken for granted in their local dating market. Mike, a frequent traveler to Colombia, had visited the country over fifteen times by 2011 in search of a girlfriend. He convinced his close friend Peter to join him on this trip, praising the safety of Medellín and the beauty of Colombian women.

Peter approached the trip more casually, while Mike was fully committed to finding a woman in Colombia. Before Peter agreed to join him, Mike reassured him about the safety of traveling in Colombia and expressed his confidence in his personal safety.

> Everything here in Medellín is so relaxed. You can go out anytime here, you have so much protection. A lot of guards, a very secure city. There are certain parts of the city you don't go out to at night, but that's common sense. Every city is the same in that way. It's like that in certain cities in the U.S. too. There are definitely parts of Miami where I'm like no way. There's a lot of crazy drugs out there. I think Miami can be more dangerous than here in Medellín. You can be in Coral Gables with no problems and go to Overtown and have problems all day long. A lot of theft in Miami. There are certain areas here that Pablo [Escobar] used to help out and you can't go up there. But the rest is just fine.

For Mike, the sight of police patrolling with AK-47s only added to his sense of security while traveling in a place associated with danger. As his comments show, Mike understood that danger exists in any urban area, and he believed that security in Medellín, especially in wealthier neighborhoods, was more visible than in cities like Miami.

Racially "Dangerous" Desires

The men I interviewed during my trips to Colombia often imagined a specific physical type as the stereotypical Colombian woman: mixed Indigenous and white, curvaceous but still thin, with long brunette hair and lighter skin. Colombian women often aspire to, and men attending romance tours expect, what scholar Hilda Lloréns terms a "Maja ideal"—a light-skinned woman, with light-colored eyes (preferably blue), a Europeanized thin nose, curvy but thin frame, and long flowing straight hair.[12] Sociologist Margaret Hunter found in her study of colorism that "true femininity is still defined in relation to whiteness."[13] Within the context of Latin America, racialized understandings of beauty are often based in the ideology of blanqueamiento, or the "whitening" of the race.[14]

Feminist scholar Felicity Schaeffer-Grabiel observed a romance tour in Cali, Colombia, and noted that most of the women she interviewed invested in their bodies as a form of social mobility, often through plastic surgery.[15] Nose jobs, breast implants, and butt implants were common among these women, all aimed at achieving a Europeanized beauty ideal with curves. Institutionally and symbolically, the Colombian nation is built on aesthetic nationalism, which centers women's bodies by highlighting exaggerated breasts and buttocks.[16]

Within the United States, the current production of Latina women in the media is both culturally desirable and socially contested as consumable and dangerous, and allows the media to portray a "racialized femininity that is safe yet exotic and sexualized."[17] Feminist scholars Emily Starr and Michele Adams call the women within the international dating industry "the domestic exotic," highlighting the exoticness of women's foreign identity and how women's exoticness is redesigned to fit within the U.S. context of marriage and the traditional nuclear family through a discourse of traditional femininity.[18] Media constructions of Colombian women as passionate and highly sexual coincide with the growth of Colombian women working as sex workers both at home and abroad in places like Spain and Curaçao.[19]

Based on Colombia's racial geographies, Paisas (people from the state of Antioquia) are known for being lighter skinned and descended from European populations, whereas the coasts of Colombia are known for their Indigenous and Black populations.[20] Santiago was on his fourth tour of Medellín and the racial geographies of Colombia played an important role in his decision of preferring to meet women in Medellín versus the coastal cities of Cartagena or Barranquilla: "When I went to Cartagena, the women were not good looking, they were much too dark. I didn't go during the beauty pageant tour. And it's not a serious place, it's party, party, party! It's just awful, it's filthy, you know when I went to their

[AFA] party, they are all dark, most of them are Black!" Medellín's association with lighter-skinned women led to the belief that Paisas were the most attractive people in all of Colombia, illustrating how racialized ideas of desirability influence where men choose to search for potential wives.

None of the men imagined Colombian women as African or dark; they were picturing the Maja ideal of a light-skinned woman with long black hair and European facial features. When I met Kyle during my first romance tour, he was not part of the formal tour and was just coinciding with the tour to attend the social on his own. Unlike most of the men I met on tour, Kyle identified politically as very liberal and had worked as a teacher in Georgia for years. Despite identifying as liberal and open-minded, Kyle still described women in Colombia as more "European" than other Latina women in Central America. Kyle further elaborated on the "European-ness" of women in Medellín:

> Anyway, I really didn't know much about the Latin women, and I guess sort of misjudged South America like many Americans do. They think it's kind of like Mexico but actually this whole area, once you get past Mexico and most of Central America, where the Aztec Indian influence was, and you have the real dark-skinned people . . . actually South America has a lot of German influence and Italian and a lot of Spanish, where it's really European . . . it's like Europeans that speak Spanish and the reason they don't speak much English, from what I understand, is the history.

Most of the men on tour identified lighter-skinned women as the more attractive women in Colombia and linked places with higher incidences of Indigenous or Black populations to lesser beautiful women.

Kyle elaborated this idea of the "domestic exotic" by comparing Colombian women to women in the United States.[21] "The two women I know or three that I know from there don't look like . . . they look like very attractive Americans. They don't have the dark skin, well one of them is a little bit dark and the other two if you saw them, you would think they were from Charlotte or Dallas or something. The Latina women are really a bit like the Italian women, although a little bit more accessible like their features are a little softer but they still remind me of the Italian women." Kyle returned to Medellín numerous times and finally did find a serious relationship with a woman from Barranquilla who matched his Maja ideal.

Greg (introduced in chapter 2) was in his early fifties and divorced from a Russian woman and an American woman but was dating an American doctor back at home in Colorado. He was a very heavy-set man and relatively tall, but the young Colombian translators could not stop commenting on Greg's body size. They would continually laugh and tell me that they had never seen anyone so large in their lives before, but Greg considered himself a catch regardless of his weight. While he enjoyed dating around locally, eventually Greg wanted to expand his adventures to new horizons abroad. He originally found out about

AFA as a way to explore potential retirement locations and meet women to date at the same time. After another failed relationship, Greg booked a tour in the Philippines to scout it as a potential retirement location.

> I had just broke-up with one of my girlfriends and I thought aw shit, I'll do something different, leaving the weather and I'm not really busy, I love to see other countries, so I booked the Philippine one. And I went over there, and I was there for ten days and let's just put it this way, I had a hella of a good time in the Philippines and actually, I'd been looking for some place that's inexpensive, that's warm in the winter, that I would love to live there for like three months.

As mentioned in the previous chapter, Greg had already married a woman from Russia and had no interest in retiring in Eastern Europe.

Greg's friend told him that the Philippines could potentially be a good option, as many people speak English and it is relatively affordable. However, Greg did not like the vibe enough in the Philippines to settle there: "Someone told me that the Philippines . . . they speak English so I wouldn't have to learn a different language. But when I went over there, it was third world, trashy . . . um, no way in hell I would want to live here type of thing." While the Philippines was not an ideal fit for Greg's retirement plans, he still enjoyed his tour experience and decided to attend another tour in a different country. He looked through AFA's other tours and decided to visit Colombia: "So I got back from that trip, and I had such a blast and I thought where do I want to go next? I was looking at the next tours and one was China, one was Colombia and I thought, you know I've heard Colombian ladies are really . . . nice, beautiful, that kind of thing. So, I booked it." In between his two trips, Greg met a local girlfriend in Colorado.

Greg was given a "hall pass" by his new girlfriend at home, since he booked the trip before their relationship started. As he later explained to me, "Yeah, I mean we had a good relationship, but I wasn't madly in love with her." While in Colombia, Greg felt an immediate connection to a local woman in her early forties, Davina, whom he met at the social on Saturday night. He became infatuated with Davina and was only interested in dating her throughout the tour, as Greg considered Davina to be a successful, well-off woman who did not need his money, even though she was "older" at the age of forty: "I mean I like the young beautiful girls and this girl's forty, but she's very beautiful and her personality is awesome. She's really pretty, but what I like best about her is her personality, her smile, she's real loving and it's for all the right reasons." Greg kept discussing Davina's beauty, and the fact that she was a locally professional woman with her own money and property.

> Like I asked her, would you like to stay in Medellín, or would you like to go to the USA, where would you like to live? She said it's up to you. She

said I would be glad to be wherever you go. I mean she's not just in it to get to the USA, which you know a lot of them could be. Like she owns a condo in Bogotá and a condo in Medellín and she's the manager of a manufacturing company that sells saw machines all over the world.

Davina's financial stability and career success in Colombia assured Greg that she was genuinely interested in him versus a green card or money. Greg, like many of the men I met on tour, wanted to be loved for who they were, not what they could provide financially, but were ultimately still semi-aware they were engaging in a form of intimate geographic arbitrage.

Greg initially considered dating a woman from the Philippines, but the age and class differences became too much for him. For Greg, women in the Philippines seemed more ready to date older men out of desperation and poverty than in Colombia: "I think the women in the Philippines are more desperate. They're willing to like . . . whatever I need to do to get out of here and find someone to support me. The women in Colombia are happy with Medellín; it's nice. Most of them work and don't live in poverty, they're not out on the streets. They got problems there but they're not in disarray. I mean they're not rich, but they're not in poverty." Greg's class-based assessment of women's authenticity assumes that his relative affluence will go further with women who are in more economically precarious positions. Thus, Greg told me women's intentions seemed purer in Colombia, "Well I think women in other countries and especially Colombia, they're really . . . You know they have a good job and lots of nice toys and possessions and all that . . . I don't think they're looking for that [money]. They're just looking for a guy that's going to be real and treat them well and have a good family life." Women's seemingly more middle-class status in Colombia reassured Greg that women were genuinely into him, versus the younger and more impoverished women he met in the Philippines.

Greg really homed in on Davina's middle-class status as one of the most attractive qualities she possessed, in addition to her beautiful appearance. After meeting Davina, Greg felt like he found all that he was looking for: "I want a woman that's got a great personality, likes to laugh, smiling, happy, likes other people, loving and sexy and likes to travel and enjoys life. And wants a good home life. And she [Davina] fits all of that." Even by the end of the tour, Greg could not stop gushing about his future plans to bring Davina to his home.

I mean she needs to learn English; I need to learn Spanish. I mean I need to come back from this time apart and you know, make sure. I mean flying there . . . you know I haven't been intimate with her yet, just hugs and kisses and little things like that and going out and enjoying life. It's all well if her personality doesn't really bother me. [Laughs.] I think about the other ones, I mean I had a couple of flings while I was there with some of the other girls there. It was just pure . . . you know you're fun kind of thing, fooling around but this one is different so I would like to be with her. Spend more time with her. Make sure it's for sure, for real.

Greg's quote points to the importance of accessing women's sexual labor, as he mentions he had sexual "flings" with other girls during his initial courtship phase with Davina. When I mentioned to Greg my trip to the strip club with the other men on the trip, he laughed and talked about how he and another guy on tour went to a different strip club together to have sex, but not damage his "pure" relationship with Davina.

While excited about the possibility of establishing a relationship with Davina, he also had to end the relationship he had back at home with his doctor girlfriend. When I asked how that relationship ended, Greg explained to me that the conversation did not go well: "She's [home girlfriend] not happy. Some people told me to just wait until before you get back over [to the United States] and my daughters said no, you need to tell her right away." Greg further mentioned how his now ex-girlfriend told him that Davina was just using him for a green card. His daughters liked his local girlfriend in the United States as well and warned Greg that he was maybe moving too quickly with Davina, as they had only been dating each other for a week. Despite his daughters' concerns, Greg was intent on trying to create a long-distance relationship with Davina and planning to return later in the year. A year later when I returned to Colombia, the local office employees told me that Davina was still attending social parties in the hopes of finding a more attractive foreign partner.

Extracting Employee Labor

During the romance tour in Medellín, the party atmosphere starts immediately, thanks to the local women employees and translators. Men arrive on Thursday, and their weekend is packed with two social events held at a local banquet venue. On the day the men arrive, Xiomara, the assistant manager of the local AFA office, gives them a brief tour, pointing out where to exchange money at favorable rates and how to navigate the El Poblado area. Xiomara and the local manager, Valentina, also encourage the men to visit the mall and ensure they have formal clothing for the social parties. Valentina told me with a laugh, "You would not believe the amount of men who come here with two pairs of cargo shorts and a few polo tops for the week. This is so weird to us in Colombia, as we are always well dressed and taking good care of ourselves." A young translator, Karina, agreed with Valentina's shock and horror at the hygienic practices of the American men coming to visit: "Omg! They get so red in the face and sweat all day, don't wear deodorant and then want to go meet a girl on a date. We Colombian women want men that smell good, not stinky." As a result, the local managers and translators encourage the men to practice good hygiene and shop for more stylish clothes if they are unprepared for Colombian women's expectations.

After the mall and currency exchange tour, Xiomara takes the men to downtown Medellín to show them the Botero statues but quickly warns them not to return to this area after dark. When asked why, Xiomara explains that many drug addicts roam the downtown streets in the evening, making it unsafe at night. To reach downtown, Xiomara shows everyone how to walk to the metro station and take the subway. Medellín's metro line is one of the city's proudest achievements, as it is the only metro system in a major Colombian city. Once the downtown tour concludes, Xiomara leads the group back to the hotel, advising the men to prepare for the big party weekend ahead. I part ways with the men after downtown and return to the local office with Xiomara, conveniently located within walking distance of the hotel.

The local office occupies a commercial building that also houses a small corner store and a music studio. A guard stands at the building's entrance, controlling access, and the AFA office is on the second floor. The office is small, decorated with pictures of happy men partying at past AFA socials, along with a few photos of smiling, successful couples. A small room in the back serves as a photo studio where women joining the website have their pictures taken. Next to the studio is a red and white couch for clients, and beyond that are two desks for Valentina and Xiomara, as well as two computer stations for the translators who handle emails for the women. The office operates from 10 A.M. to 8 P.M., though Valentina sometimes stays later if men meet dates at the office. AFA protocol requires many women to meet their dates at the office to ensure everything goes smoothly.

Since it was the day before the socials, both Valentina and Xiomara were stressed out getting the final details together for the parties on Friday and Saturday night. They were both frantically calling local women in order to confirm that they were indeed coming to the socials that weekend. Valentina told me, "We have to get a lot of girls to come. If there are not a lot of girls, the guys get unhappy and complain." I stayed at the office for a while just observing the local women managers and translators hard at work, trying to corral as many women as they possibly could for the social events.

Throughout their calls, it seemed as though many women were confirming their attendance that weekend and they kept telling the local women that the party will be very fun with free food and alcohol. I asked Karina if the free food and drinks were significant incentives for women to meet the men on tour. She laughed, "Of course. You will see what happens after the dinner tomorrow. But in the meantime, it will be fun, and we will party together. Make sure to dress up." The entire office team, both managers and translators, were all younger than twenty-five years old. Most of the translators were Valentina's friends, and she hired both men and women to translate at the social parties. This arrangement sometimes caused issues with some male clients who preferred to work only with female translators.

Friday night marked the first social event. To blend in with the vibe, I dressed up in a skirt, heels, and makeup. I met the other men on tour in the hotel lobby, as the entire group was being bused to the party venue together. Valentina and Xiomara arrived in form-fitting minidresses, and the men on tour complimented them on their outfits and beauty. Like in the airline or tourist industries, the international dating industry often hires young, attractive women to work in local offices as managers and translators.[22] These women provide an aspirational figure for the men and offer insights into local women and dating practices. Women are seen as more skilled at offering emotional support, particularly to men who need help with things like clothing or hygiene.

We all climbed into minibuses and headed to the social venue, where Tim and Jimmy met us in the lobby. As tour veterans, they had rented an Airbnb apartment instead of staying at the hotel with the rest of the group. In fact, Tim and Jimmy just paid to join the social parties and planned their own independent trip alongside, but separate, from the official tour. Tim explained to me, "Look we are staying in an upscale apartment which is way better than the hotel. We just pay $50 to attend each social night and save a ton of money this way." Tim and Jimmy had been on a number of AFA tours and were ready to do the travel planning on their own, but still wanted to meet women at the social and utilize the services the local staff provide. As we entered the venue, I noticed that the room was set up with fifteen individual tables and a group of women were seated at each table. A bar area was set up in a corner opposite the tables, with a couch and separate table for the local AFA employees, as well as a large area cleared out to create a dance floor. I walked in with Valentina and Xiomara to sit at the employee table, and as I walked through the room, all the women attendees looked at me in confusion. Valentina quickly reassured the women that I was not there to date, but simply to observe.

Before the social began, each man was assigned a translator and provided with a notebook and pen to jot down notes about the women and exchange contact information. The eleven men on the tour, plus a few others who had paid only for the social, were each seated at separate tables, surrounded by six to eight women and their translators. I quickly realized the event followed a speed-dating format, where participants rotated tables every few minutes to meet everyone in the room. AFA promotes these social events as a fast and efficient way for men to meet hundreds of women in a short time. For the first hour, the men moved from table to table, meeting all the women. Then a banquet crew served dinner, and the men remained at their last table, allowing for more intimate conversations with the women seated there.

While men had been purchasing drinks at the cash bar throughout the evening, the free aguardiente was specifically for the local women to help them relax and enjoy the party.[23] Despite the free liquor, I noticed that many women left the event after dinner. Often, women who are not interested in that particular group of foreign men leave after the meal, skipping the drinking and dancing entirely. Most of the men did not seem to notice, as they were caught up in the shots, dancing, and the women who remained. The DJ started playing reggaetón, and the women who stayed gravitated to the dance floor and the bar for more aguardiente.

The group of translators and office employees joined in, drinking shots and dancing together, clearly enjoying themselves. After about an hour of dancing and drinks, the social began to wind down. The venue was rented for only three hours, but many men did not want the night to end, just like in Ukraine. Some of the men made plans to head to nightclubs in the El Poblado area with women they had met at the social. At the time, the most popular nightclub for tourist men was Mango's, known for its U.S. Western theme, go-go dancers, and performers who are little people. As one of the largest nightclubs in Latin America, Mango's was a common after-party spot for men and women once the social ended at 11 P.M. As plans were made for the evening, the translators said their goodbyes. They were done working for the night, even if the men continued to clubs with women. From that point on, the men would have to rely on their own communication skills or Google Translate.

After the social, I went out with Xiomara and Karina to Parque Lleras for more drinks and to discuss the event's success. Xiomara was pleased that the food and alcohol had been sufficient and that a good number of women attended. Both she and Valentina wanted to avoid complaints, and Xiomara was relieved that the first social party was well attended. She was also glad that some of the men continued the night at Mango's and other clubs. The more fun the men had, the fewer complaints and requests Xiomara would have to handle. She remarked, "Well, if the guys meet girls at the social, then our week setting up dates for them will be less busy." For the women who work at the local office, happy and entertained men clients made their jobs a lot easier.

The morning after the social, I had breakfast with the men staying at the hotel. So far, they had a positive impression of Colombian women and their tour experience. The group met again in the hotel lobby to be driven together to the next social event. Valentina and Xiomara arrived early to escort the men and ensure everything went smoothly. The men were excited and energized by the attention they received from the women in Colombia, eagerly taking their seats at tables where women were already waiting.

However, some men who were assigned male translators expressed frustration. A few complained to me that having a young, attractive local man as their translator made them feel uneasy. One common concern was that the local women seemed to flirt with the male translators, likely due to their ability to communicate in Spanish, leaving the foreign men feeling sidelined. Tim whispered to me, "These guy translators are a terrible idea. Thank God mine isn't." Beyond this perceived competition, I noticed that the men often expected emotional support from the female managers and translators, relying on them for guidance and encouragement.

The gender dynamics of translating became evident during my interviews with the men. Many expressed that they only wanted to work with female employees, especially in the roles of translators or office managers. After this tour, the local manager had to fire the male translators because too many men complained to the head office in Phoenix, saying it was inappropriate to have young, attractive men as translators and potential competitors.

Xiomara explained that men often turned to her and Valentina for various forms of emotional support, asking for advice on local women, dating expectations, and even fashion. The translators, too, became personal confidantes for the men, providing a significant amount of emotional labor. One translator, Elisa, was deeply involved in the success of a relationship I witnessed during my time in Medellín. She had been assigned to Larry on his first tour in Colombia and continued to help him communicate with Carolina, the woman he became serious about. Even outside of her official duties, Elisa continued to assist the couple, meeting with them as Carolina took English lessons and helping them during Larry's visits. Elisa's experience highlights the deep emotional bonds translators can form with both the men and women clients, sometimes becoming deeply invested in the relationships they help to cultivate.

Conclusion

Throughout the romance tour experience, U.S. men often extract various forms of labor from local women, including aesthetic, sexual, intimate, and emotional labor. Many of the men I interviewed perceived Colombia as a dangerous yet alluring place, filled with attractive and sexually skilled women. Some openly engaged with sex workers, whether in strip clubs or brothels, while simultaneously searching for what they considered "pure" love. These men saw no contradiction in dating women without engaging in sex to keep those relationships "pure" while satisfying their sexual desires with local sex workers. In this way, they extracted aesthetic, intimate, and emotional labor from the women they dated, sexual labor from the women they paid, and emotional labor from the translators and local agency managers.

The men on tour in Colombia often felt empowered by traveling to a destination associated with danger, kidnapping, and drug trafficking. They relished the opportunity to boast about their travels and exploits to friends and family back home, who were often fearful of visiting Colombia. This sense of bravery boosted their sense of masculinity, as did the various forms of labor they extracted from the women they encountered. For these men, Colombia represented a frontier of fun, sex, drugs, and danger, where they could pursue a particular mixed-race ideal of womanhood while asserting their masculinity.

5

Philippines

The Frontier of Marriage

Within the contemporary international dating industry, the Philippines serves as the frontier of serious relationships and marriage, where Western men go to extract care and aesthetic labor from local women. Narratives about Filipino women tend to focus in on their "caring" labor and skills. Men I interviewed would mention Filipinas' backgrounds in nursing and the amount of care labor women performed for men they were dating. Anthropologist Nicole Constable observed in her comparative study of brides in the Philippines and China that the American men she interviewed characterized Filipino women as more demure, conservative, and in need of rescue in comparison to Chinese women.[1] Men's extraction of women's care labor, as well as their intimate and aesthetic labors, is predicated on the more than century-long colonial and postcolonial relationship between the Philippines and the United States.

The Philippines' role as a labor-exporting state in the global economy also shapes Western men's perceptions of Filipino women's reproductive, intimate, and care labor.[2] Unlike Medellín or various cities in Ukraine, the men I interviewed did not express a strong affinity for Davao in the Philippines. Despite being the country's third-largest city, Davao is not known for its beaches or shopping. Most men on the romance tour stayed at the Marco Polo Hotel, the only high-end hotel in Davao, and avoided venturing out for food or entertainment. Some men mentioned that witnessing the poverty was too depressing, so they preferred to stay at the hotel. Despite their mixed feelings about Davao, the men consistently praised Filipino women's conservative family values and their association with care labor, such as nursing or domestic work.

Throughout the tour, men extracted aesthetic, emotional, intimate, and sexual labor from both the women they dated and those working as translators and managers for the agency. In Colombia, men openly discussed their access to sex workers, but in the Philippines, those stories were kept quiet if they participated.

In Davao, where men pursued more serious dating relationships, Filipino women provided aesthetic labor by being attractive and thin, intimate labor through touch, and care labor by offering emotional support and physical care, which helped boost the men's self-esteem and masculinity.

Men who felt ignored or underappreciated in their local dating markets often remarked on the noticeable boost in attractiveness they experienced in the Philippines, where they felt relatively wealthy. This chapter examines men's understanding of the Philippines as a postcolonial frontier of marriageable women, the ways poverty shapes men's perceptions of women's authenticity, and the narratives surrounding young Filipino women's accessible care and aesthetic labor. The search for significantly younger women is a key factor, as many men travel to the Philippines specifically looking for women willing to accept large age gaps, such as a forty-year difference. While women in Ukraine and Colombia were much less likely to date or marry men more than fifteen years older, large age gaps with foreign men are more normalized in the Philippines. The men I interviewed consistently cited Filipino women's acceptance of these large age gaps as a major reason for choosing to attend a romance tour in the Philippines.

The Philippines: The Postcolonial Frontier

Buck, a longtime tour leader and employee of A Foreign Affair (AFA), explained that while Ukraine is the most popular tour destination, the Philippines is quickly gaining in popularity. He attributes this rise to Filipinas' English-speaking abilities, which stem from the colonial and postcolonial relationship between the Philippines and the United States. The Spanish–American War of 1898 presented the United States with a new frontier after achieving its "Manifest Destiny" by conquering the western coast of the continental United States. Following the defeat of Spain in the war, the United States occupied the Philippines for fifty years, suppressing local Filipino independence fighters.[3]

The United States initiated a mission to educate Filipinos in the American way of life. This effort included establishing a public education system, a massive undertaking that involved recruiting and sending between 600 and 1,000 American teachers to the Philippines to teach English and literacy. Feminist historian Teresita C. del Rosario argues that the American colonial experience in the Philippines was more about seduction than the imposition of values. The influence of this colonial mission persists today, as English is widely spoken, and American ideas about color and race remain influential.[4]

Economic development was another major American imperial goal in the Philippines, benefiting American capitalists along the way. While the United States provided improved infrastructure, its colonial economic and trade policies ultimately hindered the Philippines' long-term economic development. World War II marked the end of direct American colonialism and occupation in the Philippines—first through Japanese occupation and then, after the war, official political independence from both Japan and the United States. However, special legal privileges for American citizens, businesses, and even the U.S. military remain in place, despite the closure of military bases in Angeles City and Subic Bay and their transformation into free trade zones.[5]

Neoliberal Migrants

The Philippines had a long history of migration to various countries around the world before the dictatorship of the infamous Ferdinand Marcos, but his regime accelerated, formalized, and encouraged this migration.[6] The largest migrant flow of overseas workers in the world is still from the Philippines, and the government relies heavily on the income these migrants remit through legal channels.[7] A significant portion of these migrants are women working as domestic workers. Thus, sociologist Rhacel Parreñas calls Filipinas the "quintessential workers of globalization" and the "global servants of capitalism."[8] The state's encouragement of labor migration helps address unemployment and underemployment at home, yet migrant workers face contradictory social mobility: they may earn higher wages but often experience a decline in social status upon migrating.

The majority of Filipino women labor migrants immigrate to the Middle East and East Asian countries, with smaller groups migrating to the United States, Canada, Australia, and Europe.[9] According to the most recent numbers from the Philippine Statistics Authority in 2022, the number of Overseas Filipino Workers (OFWs) is 2.16 million, over half of that workforce (1.2 million or 55.6 percent) are women).[10] Most OFWs are heading toward Asia (77.4 percent), with 20 percent of OFWs headed to Saudi Arabia. Large percentages also migrate for work to in the United Arab Emirates (13.6 percent), Kuwait (6.5 percent), Hong Kong (6.4 percent), and Singapore (3.9 percent). Saudi Arabia, Singapore, Japan, and Taiwan all have strict regulations regarding Filipinos' work contracts, which include prohibitions against marriage to local citizens, bringing their families, or gaining legal residency status. Numerous scholars have discussed the fact that many Filipino women migrants attempt to marry local men in order to secure more permanent resident status in places like Japan and South Korea.[11]

Feminist scholars like Lisa Law and Teresita del Rosario connect the development of the contemporary sex tourism industry in the Philippines to the history of American colonialism and militarism.[12] In the city of Olongapo, near Subic Bay Naval Base, numerous women worked as hostesses and sex workers for decades servicing American navy members. Angeles City, which is next to the Clark Air Force Base, developed a reputation as a center of sex work for American servicemen too. Although both bases officially closed in the 1990s and converted to special economic zones, sociologist Victoria Reyes argues that these areas have become global borderlands where multiple sets of laws apply and no clear sovereignty exists.[13] Due to this history of military sexual colonialism, an active sex tourism industry developed in Angeles City and Subic Bay. The U.S. ambassador to the Philippines, Harry Thomas Jr., created a wave of controversy in 2011 when he claimed that nearly 40 percent of male tourists traveling to the Philippines are traveling there for sexual adventures.[14]

Unlike Colombia, sex work in the Philippines is technically illegal, but most law enforcement tolerates it in certain red-light districts.[15] Although the Philippines is a popular destination for sex tourists, it is overshadowed by Thailand in Southeast Asia and is more commonly associated with migrants and mail order brides.[16] Nicole Constable observed that American men's fantasy of Filipino women is more aligned with fairy tale notions of romance, since international dating industry representations of Filipinas depend on their innocence and respectability versus the overt sexualized representations of Russian and Ukrainian women.[17] In her book about the international dating industry, she argues, "Like the Disney Cinderella, prospective Filipina brides are often represented as poor, innocent young women who deserve to be rescued from menial labor and shabby clothes by way of marriage to a Western hero prince."[18] Many dating agency websites focus on Filipino women as petite, slender, feminine, pious, hardworking, and respectable, rather than emphasizing their sexuality. The men I interviewed echoed these narratives, highlighting Filipinas' traditional values, hard work despite poverty, and adherence to religion as qualities that set them apart from the more overtly sexualized women in Colombia and Ukraine.

Poverty, Conservative Values, and Questions of Authenticity

Halia, the owner of the local affiliate matchmaking agency, worked for a major transnational corporation before opening her agency in Davao. She coordinated with the main AFA office in Phoenix to organize romance tours, while her business partner ran the Cebu office for AFA. AFA chose not to open its own offices in the Philippines due to strict laws against the mail order bride industry and human trafficking and opted to use Halia and her partner as affiliates on the ground.[19] Halia's experience in the corporate world exposed her to many politicians, enabling her to navigate the laws regulating the industry.

Unlike the tour sites I visited in Colombia and Ukraine, Davao City appeared more impoverished, even in its wealthier areas. Located on the island of Mindanao, far from Manila, Davao is impacted by ongoing separatist conflicts with the federal government. There have been bombings in Davao, including one at the airport in 2003 and another at a night market in 2016. As a result, Mindanao is on the U.S. State Department's travel advisory list, though Davao City itself is considered relatively safe.

During my time in Davao, I noticed stricter rules compared to other Philippine cities. Rodrigo Duterte, the former president of the Philippines, served as mayor of Davao for five terms. His daughter, Sara Duterte, the current vice president, was the mayor during my visit in 2012. Rodrigo Duterte implemented a law-and-order approach to combat terrorism, and many locals I met in Davao remained strong supporters of the Duterte family. They often questioned the international media's portrayal of Duterte's drug war and his controversial comments about women and drug users.

While following the romance tour, I spent a day with several employees at a beach resort on Samal Island. When I asked about the mayor of Davao, everyone eagerly praised the Duterte family's leadership. Layla and Veronica, two employees I spent time with at the movies and the mall, credited the Davao Death Squad for saving the city from crime. Layla, a local employee in her mid-twenties, explained, "The really bad criminals, like murderers, rapists, drug dealers, Duterte lets them out of prison and gives them twenty-four hours to leave the city. If they don't, the Davao Death Squad finds and kills them. And this is great because now our city doesn't have crime or problems." When I questioned whether vigilante justice was a good idea, most employees agreed that the Death Squad was essential to the Duterte family's success in making Davao safer. When Duterte won the election for president, the majority of my participants remained strong supporters of his war on drugs and other policies.

Most of the men I met on tour in the Philippines felt safe and instead were more struck by the poverty that they witnessed. Leon, a fifty-eight-year-old, divorced engineer from Missouri, was truly disturbed by the level of poverty that he was witnessing in Davao, and recognized his stay at the four-star hotel in the center of town was unlike most average Filipinos' daily experiences: "It's been like, two different tracks of the same train. Two rails. I'm seeing the lifestyle of the people when I rode in from the airport—there's the world of Marco Polo [hotel] and then there's the tour. There's two separate things going on at the same time." He mentioned to me that while he was expecting some unease upon his arrival in the Philippines, he was shocked at what he perceived as intense poverty: "I knew there would be a culture shock, but I didn't realize to what a degree of, how poor it would be. I came from the airport to here, and that was a pretty stark first impression."

Leon explained to me that the poverty he saw in Davao was unlike anything that people in the United States experience: "A lot of these girls, come from, you've seen the poverty here. When I got off the bus to go to the hotel, I had no idea how important money was here . . . people are poor and we're not talking down on your luck, we're talking ruinous poverty." Leon was so disturbed by the poverty that he largely refused to leave the hotel unless it was for an agency-sponsored excursion. After getting food poisoning at an off-site restaurant, he decided to stick to eating and going on dates at the Marco Polo Hotel.

Mikey and Tom are brothers that both divorced after long marriages and found romance tours to be a good option for meeting new women. During my interview with them both, Tom praised Filipino women, and women in other romance tour locations, for appreciating the small luxuries in life based on their impoverished living conditions: "Here, these girls don't have nothing. They live in a house with no walls. Similar in Colombia and Russia. You bring one of these girls home and take an American woman down there and drop her off and send her to one of the shanties or slums that they got here, it's like they couldn't make it." Tom argued that women from poorer situations are more accommodating in general than women in the United States.

> I'll tell you what. I met a woman at the social, she lives an hour away. After the social was done, I was like you can come stay with me. She didn't bring any clothes for the Eden excursion [the next day]. You can't wear this dress and shoes, so she said I have to go home now. I said would you like to go home and come back in the morning, or would you like to stay and get up early and come back? She goes I will just stay with you and get up at 4. It's safer at that time of the day. She left and got back on time for the Eden excursion.

While some men found the poverty in the Philippines too depressing, Tom and his brother believed it made women stronger, more mature, and more grateful, in contrast to what Tom described as "spoiled" American women.

Despite viewing Filipinos as sweeter and more conservative, Jay, a middle-aged small business owner on his first tour, expressed concerns to me about potential scams: "You gotta be careful here [in the Philippines] cause a lot of women try to extract money to create a better future." Jay assessed that accessing women's intimate, emotional, and sexual labor comes at a potential cost. However, as I mentioned in a previous publication, men typically defined Filipinas as more honest and less likely to engage in scams than women in Ukraine.[20] For example, Jay explained to me, "I think these ladies here [the Philippines] are much more trustworthy [compared to Ukrainian women]. Here another girl that I was dancing with, you know, I could feel her hands—she was nervous. She was very nervous, so, ok this is really sweet, she was kind of shaky, you know." Jay found reassurance in the nervousness of the women, believing it indicated genuine intentions to find a serious relationship.

Besides finding most of the women to be on the more sincere and sweet side, Jay pointed to what he saw as the tighter-knit family unit in the Philippines: "Yeah, the family seems to be tighter there, you know, mothers and fathers, a lot of mothers and fathers still together. So, I ask these girls how their parents still love each other and most of them are still happy. It's kinda interesting, so in America, it's 50% worse." Thus, Jay figured his best bet in terms of finding a younger woman willing to perform the emotional, reproductive, sexual, and intimate labor of raising a family was to attend a romance tour in the Philippines.

Despite Jay's belief that Filipinos held more conservative values related to family and gender norms, he still was cautious about finding a woman within the international dating industry. Jay explained to me that some of the other international dating websites seemed less reputable and more likely to contain potential "scammers."

> Oh god. Oh yeah, that's pretty much the whole thing. Like the company [blanked out], I would see all kinds of crap, like could you send me 50 dollars for a webcam so you can see me, and I can see you. They always say don't send money, I understand with difficult times, can you send me 30 dollars to pay for expenses, which for us is nothing, but down here it's a lot of money. I mean they are on the camera, saying "Hi Jay," and I can't send you a picture because my camera's broken and they are really a guy. I have seen many guys that look like girls and thought, "is that a girl?" And then they're really guys.

While the idea of scams is a recurring theme in the international dating industry, most men characterized women in the Philippines as less likely to engage in financial scams, especially when meeting in person at social events, compared to email correspondence and video chat on some websites.

Young and Accessible Labor

The main appeal of the Philippines for many men on romance tours is the opportunity to connect with significantly younger women who embody traditional femininity. While sitting in the lobby of the Marco Polo Hotel in Davao, I watched Jared pace anxiously for hours. Jared, a wiry, shorter man in his sixties with a full head of gray hair, had come to the Philippines in search of his third wife. Despite the many women he could have met, Jared only had eyes for one: Marielle, a nineteen-year-old he met at the tour's first social event. She was taller than him and very thin, and Jared was completely smitten.

During a conversation on the rooftop patio the night before, Jared had shared his past. He married his first wife, a sixteen-year-old Latina woman, with her parents' permission when he was in his early twenties. After a few children, the marriage ended, and he later married another significantly younger woman. When that marriage also failed, Jared turned to online dating and discovered AFA's website. He told me he was drawn to the Philippines by the women's conservative Christian values and lifestyles.

While conservative values, women's available labor, and femininity capital played a significant role in men's decision to attend romance tours in the Philippines, several men based their decision on Filipino women's willingness to accept much larger age gaps between themselves and their husbands than in the other AFA countries. Jared, clearly thrilled by his connection with Marielle, compared her to his previous wives as we sat having drinks. He gushed about how she was more beautiful and traditional than either of them. "I just want to take Marielle back home to California with me," he said. "I have the time and money to do fun things, and she seems like the perfect companion for me." When I asked about the significant age difference, Jared dismissed it, saying, "Age is just a number. It's how you feel that matters. Besides, I'm still open to having children." This desire for children was common among the men I interviewed in the Philippines.

However, on Jared's last day in Davao, he paced frantically in the hotel lobby, waiting to hear from Marielle. Unlike most men on the tour, Jared had focused solely on her, despite AFA's encouragement to date multiple women to avoid getting too attached to one person. He had broken that rule because he was so enamored with Marielle. As he stood waiting, I approached him to check in. Jared, on the verge of tears, said, "I can't get ahold of Marielle. She's not answering her phone, and she was supposed to see me before I leave for the airport. I wanted to give her a ring to show my commitment, and now she's not here." I reassured him that there might be a misunderstanding, but Marielle never contacted him. Jared eventually accepted that she was not ready to take their relationship to the next level, but as he prepared to leave the hotel, he looked devastated.

While Jared's pursuit of Marielle did not work out, eleven out of the nineteen men on the tour ended up engaged by the end of the week. The engagement rate on tours in the Philippines is notably high compared to those in Colombia and Ukraine. When I expressed my surprise, Halia, the local owner, explained that such high engagement rates were the norm. She provided the men with detailed information about visa requirements for bringing fiancées and wives to the United States, Australia, Canada, and Western Europe, and she had facilitated the process for many clients. My observations of these high engagement and marriage rates are supported by United States Citizenship and Immigration Services data, which shows that nearly 20 percent of K-I fiancé visas filed in most years come from the Philippines.[21] This makes the Philippines the most marriage-oriented romance tour destination, shaped by the American view of the country as a familiar postcolonial frontier.

Early the next morning, after the social event, all the men, their dates, and I gathered in the Marco Polo Hotel lobby to board a bus to a chartered boat. The beaches in Davao are heavily polluted, so tourists often travel by boat to Samal Island to find pristine white sand beaches. Our group visited Paradise Resort, the most exclusive spot on the island. The men spent the afternoon with their dates, enjoying the beach, drinks, food, and jet ski rides. The women lavished attention on the men, offering massages and affection.

Tom and Mikey had come on the excursion. Tom brought a date he met at the social party and Mikey brought his employee buddy Layla as his date. Layla, as a heavier-set woman, was one of the employees not listed as a profile on the website, and typically Halia did not encourage unlisted employees to date clients. Layla also had a long-term local Filipino boyfriend at the time. However, Layla accepted the date with Mikey and went on this excursion with him to see what a foreign man could offer. Halia was fine with the situation since Mikey begged for Layla to accompany him. Tom had been encouraging Mikey to ask Layla out as soon as she was assigned to him as a translator and "buddy," as both were heavier-set men. Tom explained to both of us that Layla was the more appropriate size for men of a certain weight: "Mikey won't break Layla. Now, a hundred-pound girl? Maybe!" Despite Tom's larger size and advice to his brother, he was still going on dates with mostly petite women weighing under 120 pounds.

After their dates, both brothers were amazed at the amount of attention and caring labor they received from women they barely knew. Mikey told me, "You know what? I was at the beach yesterday and I must say I took my buddy [Layla], and she is a beautiful young woman, 30 years old. And when I'm looking at some of these other guys out there in the water with these women, or not necessarily in the water, on these excursions, I haven't had a woman who supposedly loved me treat me better than these women treat these men." Tom then interjected, "On a second date! But women here are attentive and in Peru and in Colombia too. They all are attentive, but American women are not attentive. And my attentiveness is not reciprocated. It's never reciprocated." Both Mikey and Tom felt ignored by women in their local dating markets and believed that romance tours gave them a better chance to meet quality women, especially younger women, who were still willing to provide the emotional and intimate labor that they believed American women no longer offered.

Tom consistently commented on men's ability to access women's labor and femininity capital from women much younger than themselves, particularly for men in their fifties and sixties: "There's a guy here I can't help but notice. He's older, heavyset, in shorts. I saw him in the elevator with a woman who must be around 30, she might be 30, and he's probably 65. What do you think when you see something like that?" After I explained to Tom that age differences did not bother me, but that I was not interested in pursuing a relationship with a man my father's age, Tom responded, "Rules like that [about appropriate age differences] were made to be broken. If you grow up seeing a large age difference like that it's normal. It's all cultural. We get better looking the richer we get." Tom's comment also points to men's recognition that economic considerations influence women's assessments of men's attractiveness, especially when searching for a younger woman.

Mikey, Tom's brother, shared a story about a successful couple with a large age gap, where the woman was from outside the United States: "See, I did a job for this man, about 8 or 9 years ago, and he was out on a [oil] rig in the middle of nowhere. He was probably 65 years old and his wife might have been 33. She loved that guy! I have no doubt in my mind. She was out there, in the middle of nowhere, 100 miles from the nearest shoe store. She loved that guy. She was from Mexico." Mikey agreed with his brother that large age differences are common in non-Western cultures and that women from outside of the United States are more likely to provide the traditional forms of emotional and reproductive labor that men in the industry often seek out, such as moving to uncomfortable places to provide their husbands with reproductive and emotional forms of labor.

Davis, a fifty-three-year-old business owner from Ohio, felt his masculinity boosted by the attention he received from young, beautiful women in the Philippines—something he rarely experienced in the United States. When I asked if dating was easier in the Philippines compared to his local market, he replied, "Yes, it is. It is hard to imagine that coming from a society where a woman of such beauty and magnitude would not give me a second glance. At least that's the impression I get." Davis felt invisible and ignored by women in the United States, a sentiment echoed by many men I interviewed. Emboldened by his newfound desirability, Davis explained his preference for younger women: "To be honest I had somewhere in the back of my mind, 35 would have been the lowest. After having been here [the Philippines] they [women aged thirty-five and older] don't look at me, the scale doesn't work the same. See, my thing was to try to find a woman who looked 35 to be 35. I'm not going to stereotype them but it looks like they've been ridden rough and put away wet, a lot of them, so it's not their fault." Like many men, Davis defended his choice of younger women, believing that poverty in the Philippines aged women both in appearance and maturity. For him, it was about finding women who did not show signs of hardship, highlighting the importance of aesthetic appeal in his assessment of potential wives.

Daniel, from chapter 2, shared his dating experiences after divorcing a wife who no longer wanted to be intimate due to illness. His story focused on the "baggage" older women with children carried in the United States, which made them less appealing to him: "I was dating a girl who was a nurse practitioner, she was lovely, a bit younger than I was and she had a twenty-six-year-old son who was autistic on a low functioning level and she was never going to put him in a halfway house where he can learn to be alone and a normal person. She was like no, he will always live with me. That was too much for me." Daniel found that women his age often came with challenges, making their labor less accessible to him. By seeking a younger Filipina, he hoped to avoid the complications he associated with older women.

Daniel's interest in Filipino women was also influenced by his friend's successful marriage to a Filipina. Daniel traveled to Davao to meet two women, both under twenty-five, with whom he had been corresponding for months. On the first night of the social, Halia invited Riley, one of the women Daniel had been talking to. Despite months of correspondence, Riley showed little interest in Daniel and avoided him during the event. Daniel felt the lack of interest immediately. Despite his numerous attempts to spend time with her, Riley largely avoided him to hang out with me and the other employees of the agency on the veranda to have a few drinks.

Melanie attended the social party the second night. Daniel felt an immediate connection with Melanie, despite their over twenty-year age gap, and moved full force ahead in pursuing a serious relationship with her: "But she's a third-year student, going to be a teacher. Well, she tells me that age does not matter, well I know that. But in the United States, it looks a little different. So, I kept an open mind, she's wonderful and smart and wants a family." Daniel recognized that in the United States their age gap is unusual, but he wanted to ensure his possibility of having more children.

A few days into dating, Daniel had already met all of Melanie's family: "She has a wonderful family, she took me to her house. That's like a whoa, you know? Her brother and her cousin are in the air conditioning business here, so I went to Samal Island, and they are second generation on the island. Her family was wonderful." Despite assurances from Melanie and her family about the age difference, Daniel wanted to ensure their comfort with it: "And I asked them specifically, 'I am in my late 40s, does that matter?' And they were like no, no! I'm like ok, I'm good with that." After receiving their approval, Daniel began seriously considering an engagement with Melanie.

When I asked Daniel if Melanie would finish her schooling and work in the United States, he explained to me that she could simply start working for his HVAC business instead: "She can help me at my place, work with me. If she wants to help, I don't care. If you love your partner and like your partner, it works well." He also discussed his plans to send money to her family, acknowledging the importance of filial piety in Filipino culture, something well-documented by scholars of Filipino migrants:[22] "What you got to understand is that when you marry a Filipino, you marry the whole family. I mean you're expected to send them money if you can. I have no problem with that. I mean, I think right now, three hundred dollars a month is very comfortable for them. If you don't have it, you don't have it but if you have it, it's not that big a deal." Daniel, like Tom and Mikey, understood that remittances to Filipino families would likely be part of his married life.

Jay, a fifty-four-year-old engineer from Orange County, California, compared the women in his local dating pool to those on the show *Real Housewives of Orange County*, implying they were vapid, shallow, and focused solely on money. Like many men I interviewed, Jay felt invisible in his local dating market as an older man: "Oh, boy, you know, at 54, well, you know, I just came from Orange County, Orange County Housewives. Right down the street from me and, you know, there's no interest in me, you know, very interested in money, I guess, but there's nobody that I was interested or would be interested in." For Jay, access to younger women was the main motivating factor for him to attend a tour in the

Philippines: "I always think about that age difference, that's part of the reason I came here. At my age I don't want somebody my age, which is no problem. I want to enjoy myself. That's the truth." Like most men I interviewed, Jay's desire to marry a much younger woman influenced his decision to join the romance tour.

A self-identified workaholic engineer, Jay spent time corresponding with women from the website ahead of his trip to the Philippines: "I wrote a bit, I did it like maybe a month in advance. So, I was in love with this 24-year-old woman, and she wanted at least some time to get to know me. It's a little strange to meet somebody right away and get married, like a 54-year-old guy and a 24-year-old woman." Despite Jay's preference for significantly younger women than himself, he still claimed he was looking for a deep intellectual connection: "I just don't want somebody that it's just gonna be boring. You get to a certain point in your life and you just wanna have intellectual conversation." When I asked him if his new twenty-four-year-old Filipino girlfriend was highly educated and ready for those types of conversations, Jay replied, "She's . . . she's, yeah. That's the thing I've been struggling with. . . . She's 24 and she's in a hotel management [program], student, it's like she's still a student." Despite stating the importance of intellectual connection, Jay's desire for youth ultimately outweighed his concern for deep conversations in his relationship.

Not all of the men I met in the Philippines wanted a woman considerably younger than themselves. Belinda, the announcer/emcee at the social events, was planning to leave the Philippines with her fiancé Charles at the end of his trip to Davao. We met in the agency office on the afternoon of the first social and Charles was seated next to me at the social event later that evening. Relatively young compared to the median age of the tour participants at thirty-two years old, Charles stood out in the Philippines. Charles also was unique in the sense that he did not choose to attend a tour at all; he was only at the social event as Halia's special guest as another example of a successful couple.

When I invited Charles out to lunch at the mall, the main place to hang out in Davao, he explained to me that the tour environment did not appear conducive to establishing a serious relationship: "I mean, I'm sure it's a fun time but if I was truly looking to meet somebody and have a serious relationship, I wouldn't expect it to happen. I'm not saying it can't happen, obviously, it can happen, but the social thing is just too many girls. You don't really get a chance to know anyone." Charles, who was into scuba diving, had considered visiting the Philippines independently to meet Belinda rather than joining a romance tour: "So that's why. I mean I looked, I saw they offered it and I just thought it wasn't for me. I'm more of an independent traveler, don't really do group tours. It's just not my thing. So yeah, I'm a little different." Charles was one of the handful men I met that was uninterested in the entire group tour experience.

When I asked why such a young man was interested in the industry, he claimed he simply was attracted to Asian women, particularly Filipinas, and found

AFA's website online while he was trying to date women online: "I don't know, I just stumbled across an AFA website through research. I was trying online dating and it's kind of how I got involved in this. I got interested in Filipino culture through a girl I met in the U.S., and I dated her for one or two years. And after I dated her, I kinda figured I would pursue finding another Filipino. And outside of that, obviously I am attracted to Filipinas. Physically, I am just attracted to Asian women." Having been engaged before, Charles was not finding anyone he was romantically interested in through his local dating markets, so he decided to join AFA's website to meet women in the Philippines: "And yeah, so I just thought I would give it a shot. I've been engaged before when I was 24. It didn't work, whatever happened, and we didn't get married. Obviously, I was only ever dating women in the U.S., and it wasn't really working, so I tried and thought I would give it a shot. And see what happens." He began looking at the profiles of women on the site and found Belinda's, as her profile was one of the first to have a video attached to it.

Charles was immediately attracted to Belinda but was not interested in corresponding with or meeting a large number of women: "Well I'm different than a lot of the guys on these tours, I think. When I came here to the Philippines, I really wanted to meet her [Belinda], I was interested in her. A few of the other ones I messaged a few times and there was really nothing there. It was three girls, maybe at first, and after a couple weeks of messages, she [Belinda] was the only one I connected with." In many ways, Charles's experience differs from the typical strategy most men adopt on these tours, where they are encouraged to meet a large number of women.

Charles planned his trip to Davao to meet Belinda around his own desire to go on vacation and scuba dive in other parts of the Philippines: "I planned on coming to the Philippines anyway on my own to go on vacation and go scuba diving. I decided it would maybe be cool to meet someone while I was already out there or if not, since I had already been out there before, I would go to Boracay and hang out by myself and go diving." The island of Mindanao, where Davao is located, is listed as Level 3 in the U.S. State Department's travel advisory for the Philippines, urging people to reconsider travel there due to "crime, terrorism, civil unrest and kidnapping."[23] Unlike the majority of the men I met during the romance tour, Charles was relatively more educated about the location and a little bit nervous traveling to Davao: "That's what I was doing [scuba diving] when I came here and I was a little nervous coming to Davao, because all you ever hear in America is about how dangerous it is. So, I went searching online about people who have traveled here and expats who lived here and they said how awesome it was here. Now that I have been here and around the Philippines, I feel way safer here than in Manila." By the end of his first trip, he began to appreciate Davao and feel relatively safe.

Charles noted that he was largely an independent traveler unlike many of the men on the tour who preferred to be catered to by the local women employees and translators: "Even Halia was like you are one of the first guys, we had a few others, it's not the usual thing. The usual thing is to have them [women employees] do everything for you. And yeah, the first time I came, if I and Belinda didn't hit it off, I don't think I would have used the office to find any other girls." While Charles was interested in dating Belinda, he was not looking for just any Filipina to marry. As a younger man, he was not interested in dating women much younger than himself: "She's [Belinda] pretty much the age limit I told myself, ten years. More than ten years, it's just too much. I will say that one thing I will say about Filipina girls versus American girls, is that she, at 23 years old, is way more mature than 23-year-olds you would meet in the U.S." Here, Charles echoed a common narrative I heard in the Philippines—that poverty accelerates maturity, making larger age gaps more acceptable: "She's more mature than half the 30-year-olds I know. Just because I think they have to deal with some much more real-life stuff, being poor. She already has life experience, so you know she's really mature from living here, she's had to fend for herself. Help send money to her family; help raise brothers and sisters." Charles associated Belinda's maturity with her experiences of poverty and filial piety, although her family was relatively well-off and did not need remittances from her anymore. However, Charles was willing to send money if her family needed help.

Extracting Employee Labor

During the romance tour in the Philippines, the atmosphere at the social events was more conservative and contained compared to those in Colombia and Ukraine. The local office owner, Halia, did not allow the women participating to drink, unlike in the other countries. On the first night, I ordered a local taxi to the venue, and Halia directed me to a large table at the head of the room. Similar to the setup in Colombia, several tables were arranged, each seating eight to ten women. With nineteen men participating in the tour, nearly one hundred local women attended both events. Most of the men were from the United States, with a few Australians and Canadians also present. Unlike other social events, Belinda served as the emcee, running the evening with a formal schedule of activities. Like the event in Colombia, it began with speed dating, where men moved from table to table, spending about five minutes with each group of women. In the Philippines, each man was assigned a local buddy to assist with translation and support them on dates throughout the week. These buddies followed the men to each table, collecting the women's phone numbers and contact information. After the speed dating portion ended, everyone shared a formal meal. During the meal, Belinda introduced the success story of Alma and Darren. Alma, seated further down the central table, stood up to share her story of finding love.

Alma was a single mother and a nurse who often went abroad to Saudi Arabia to work, leaving her daughter behind with her parents. Dressed up in a long gown, Alma stood up in front of the room to tell her fairytale story of love. In her late thirties and as an OFW, Alma had largely given up hope of finding a husband. One day, after a shopping trip with a friend, she took a taxi home in the Philippines. The driver, overhearing their complaints about dating local men, suggested they visit the agency office. He told them about his niece who had married a nice American man, and Alma decided to give it a try. Although she had a boyfriend working in Saudi Arabia, she was tired of waiting for him to get serious about marriage. She joined the website and received her first email from Darren, her future fiancé, immediately.

Darren visited Alma after a business trip to China, and her family was initially hesitant about her dating a foreigner. They wanted to meet him after their introduction at the agency office. Darren valued finding a religious woman, and Alma appreciated his responsibility and faith. She described being swept off her feet and was now only waiting for her K-1 fiancé visa to process. Alma encouraged both the men and women at the event to open their hearts to love, as joining the agency had changed her life. After Alma finished her inspiring story, Belinda introduced a series of games that encouraged interaction between men and women. Instead of promoting drinking, the social in the Philippines focused on more innocent forms of contact, with playful but suggestive games like a physical challenge where men and women paired up and had to grip a banana between their thighs. I mingled with everyone during the dancing and noticed that, unlike in Colombia and Ukraine, the night ended quietly. I did not see men trying to coax women to nightclubs or bars after the event. Most men seemed eager to rest and prepare for the second social event the following night.

The second night, I was seated at the VIP table with Belinda's fiancé, Charles, and one of the AFA owners' brothers, Rick. As the evening began, Rick and I chatted about why he was attending the social. He lived with his Filipina wife, Bea, in the Philippines, and they ran one of the local offices together. Rick explained how he started working for AFA, hosting romance tours in Ukraine, but eventually began corresponding with a woman in the Philippines. Although he had met someone else in Ukraine, he ultimately chose to meet his future wife, Bea, after a long correspondence. Despite a rocky first date—Bea spent much of it texting her worried friends—Rick felt a stronger connection with her than with the woman he met in Ukraine. He decided to get engaged after his first trip to the Philippines, moved there to manage a local office with Bea, and began the lengthy process of filing for a spousal visa (K-2) to the United States.

While observing the local office in the Philippines, I noticed it stayed open twenty-four hours a day, unlike the offices in Ukraine and Colombia, which operated for only ten hours a day with fewer employees. Rick attributed this difference to the dramatically lower minimum wage in the Philippines. He explained that the lower cost of labor allowed the office to remain open around the clock, something that was not feasible in Ukraine.

> I pay my workers here eight dollars a day. That's the minimum wage here. And that's for a 10-hour day. The workers in the United States have priced themselves out of the market. All the other countries, China, the Philippines, Latin America, everywhere, but the U.S., Canada, and the UK have priced themselves out of the market. . . . If they lowered the minimum wage, they [Western countries] could stop losing so many jobs. That's why they [AFA] can have the office open here 24 hours a day and not in Ukraine, because the minimum wage is eight dollars a day.

Rick believed that workers in the West had priced themselves out of the labor market by demanding higher wages. Even many countries in the developing world, in his view, paid too high of a minimum wage compared to the extremely low wages in the Philippines. Although I did not ask him to consider the different cost of living standards, I was struck by how he seemed to see his workers as living a decent life, despite the stark contrast between his view and the men clients' opinions about the poverty in the Philippines. Rick's role in running the office influenced his perspective on the economic viability of the wages he paid.

Many of the most popular women's profiles on the website worked at the local office since, as mentioned previously, Halia liked to prove to men clients that the most attractive women on the site are real. Riley, one of the most consistent profiles on the hotlist, told me that, "Well, Halia likes to have the most popular women from the site working at the local office so that the guys can see that we are real people. And this time I got to go to the social and have fun instead of work." I was impressed by how much Halia had planned ahead by hiring the most popular women from the site. She understood that a major complaint from men on other tours was that the women they corresponded with often did not attend social events or were not available to meet in person. By hiring these women, Halia could prove to the men visiting Davao that these were indeed real women interested in marriage.

A well-maintained woman in her late forties at the time, Halia dressed smart and looked the part of a successful entrepreneur. She had previously worked in upper management for Dole, the international fruit company, before transitioning into the matchmaking industry with high-profile connections. Highly respected by her employees and the women on the site, Halia ran the Davao office with much more involvement than other offices I observed, as it was her independent business. A few of the men who had attended tours in other countries praised Halia's efforts to maintain an orderly business model. Tom and Mikey often compared her management style to other managers in a positive light, especially Tom, who said, "Halia runs a tight ship. These girls are on time, and everything runs smoothly." Throughout my time in the Philippines, Halia received a great deal of praise for her leadership.

Due to the low minimum wage, the office ran two shifts, each managed by one of Halia's sons. Most of the translators and employees were women, with a few exceptions. The buddies who helped the men at the socials were all women and assisted throughout the week, navigating dates and acting as translators. The office also organized local excursions for the men, such as visits to Jack's Ridge Resort and Restaurant and Paradise Island Resort on Samal Island.

While observing the daily workings of the agency office, I noticed that many employees ended up marrying men they met through the website or tours. Belinda's marriage to Charles was particularly notable, as she was the hostess of the socials and a popular profile on the site. Marissa, who worked in the evenings, began dating a shy young man from Australia, and by the end of the tour, they were engaged. She moved to Australia within a year of meeting him.

Layla dated Mikey for a few months but ultimately married her local Filipino boyfriend. Everyone was surprised that Layla was dating one of the clients, as she was not listed on the site because she exceeded the weight limit of 55 kilograms (approximately 122 pounds). Riley pointed out that this was against the rules, saying, "It's like . . . actually she's [Layla] not allowed to date Mr. Mikey because she is not a profile and she is the staff, but Ma'am Halia can do nothing. That one is the number one rule. The staff that are not a profile are not allowed to date." Although Halia bent the rules for Layla, she typically encouraged only employees signed up on the website to date men seriously.

During the week after the tour, Veronica and Layla invited me to go to the movies. They were excited to see the film *A Secret Affair*, a local Filipino film about infidelity, at the local mall and have dinner after the movie. Over dinner, we began to discuss Layla's budding surprise romance with Mikey, as earlier in the tour I had gone out with Layla, her local Filipino boyfriend, and a few of the other office employees. Layla began telling me that she saw Mikey as more stable and responsible than her local boyfriend: "My boyfriend has a child. Yeah. Then Mikey has his three children too. I can see that Mikey is more responsible at the same time he's stable. Yeah, compared to my boyfriend." For Layla, she was not thinking about trying to date any of the men on tour, as she was in a serious relationship with her boyfriend, but Mikey began to display his interest in her at the excursion they had to Pearl Farm on Samal Island, which was the most upscale resort on Samal Island. She was attending the event as his buddy, and she traced the shift in their relationship to that trip: "And he [Mikey] showed me a lot of kindness, sweet; goodness and he surprised me a lot. Especially when we get along [chuckles] at the Pearl Farm, we have a lot of talks. We get along. That's the time that I realized then that I like this guy." After the Pearl Farm excursion, Mikey began to pursue Layla more seriously and she began having fights with her local boyfriend.

Veronica felt a bit jealous that Layla found someone, especially since she was one of the local office employees who had a profile on the site. Petite and tiny, Veronica made her dresses and outfits because finding clothes that fit her small frame was difficult. While Layla had a local Filipino boyfriend, Veronica did not date local men. At thirty, she was still a virgin and came from a religious Jehovah's Witness family. Being the youngest child and the only girl, she was surrounded by overprotective men. Working at the local office and signing up on the website gave Veronica a taste of freedom.

Earlier in the week, a group of employees, including Veronica, went to a local bar. She invited Leon, a fifty-eight-year-old divorced engineer from Missouri who was shocked by the poverty in the Philippines, to join them. I was there with Riley and could tell that Veronica was interested in Leon but too shy and inexperienced to know how to act. While eating a plate of sisig, Veronica tried to flirt with Leon, but it was clear he did not pick up on her interest or feel comfortable with it.[24] However, she did get her first kiss from Leon that evening: "Actually my first kiss is Leon. First time to hold my hand is Leon, but he was scared. Well, it's okay. Maybe it's my lesson learned. I don't know." Veronica's lack of experience with men intimidated Leon, even though he had been in a long and loveless marriage with his Chinese ex-wife: "Being the first guy is so much pressure. I don't think I can handle that." Leon felt intimidated by Veronica's inexperience. While Leon wanted a conservative woman, he did not want to be the one to teach her everything about sex. For Veronica, sex and sexuality seemed dangerous, as many people she knew got pregnant young, which is why she wanted to stay a virgin until marriage. After we finished eating at the mall, Layla and Veronica walked me to my hotel and headed home in a jeepney.

The emotional labor women employees invested in dating men from the site extended beyond just them. The entire office staff played a role in cultivating successful relationships and marriages. Halia's youngest son, Mateo, was a recent college graduate and managed the night shift with his then-girlfriend Zena. Mateo explained their role as facilitators for couples: "Like we're eliminating language barriers between the men and the women." In addition, Mateo saw their role as facilitating the tour experience for men: "We tried to assist them [the men clients] [with] things like, where to go, where to take a date but some of the things that they do is personal." Mateo traced Western men's interest in Filipino women to their better efforts at taking care of men: "Women here really take good care of the husband. As long as the husband takes good care of their wife. Give the needs. Love, affection . . ." Mateo and Zena commented that men from various Western countries, including the United States, shared their frustration with what appeared to be Western women's lack of intimate and emotional labor.

Zena also highlighted the training that Halia and the office staff provided. She pointed out that men's success depended on their approach to women and making sure the women felt taken care of. She explained that addressing men's approach was part of the training Halia gave when they arrived at the Davao office: "The guys already know how to approach the girl. Because Ma'am Halia will talk to the guy. Will talk to the guy about . . . What is the appropriate way. . . . Ma'am Halia do an orientation to the guy before they meet the girls where she explains what they like." Beyond Halia's initial training, the men's assigned buddies coached them on appearance, approach, and Filipino courting norms. These forms of emotional and intimate labor, often unrecognized as labor, were a key part of many women employees' experiences at the agency.

Conclusion: Finding Young and Accessible Labor

The Philippines has become a frontier for marriage, largely due to the availability of young women's reproductive, aesthetic, intimate, and sexual labor. Globally, Filipinas are often associated with intimate labor and care work, as many work as nurses, domestic workers, nannies, and hostesses. Men on tour often reinforced these stereotypes, pointing out the high number of Filipino nurses in the United States as evidence that they make good wives. Older men, in particular, found this association appealing.

Halia traced the success of her office's engagement rates to Filipinas' family values and English language skills: "They [men clients] like the women in the Philippines because of the culture, we are more family oriented, and more of a Christian country. Second is the communication advantage we have. English is a plus for women in the Philippines so it's easier to communicate." Halia's enormous success as a matchmaker drew many women to the agency office and word of mouth was her most successful advertising to local women: "More on the word of mouth. It is more effective. When they see their friends' successful relationships, they want that too. So, they come and become a member. Word of mouth is number one advertising." The high engagement success rate in the Philippines has made the country the most popular site for marriages within the industry.

Many men felt empowered by their relative affluence in the Philippines, often commenting that they could help "save" women and their extended families from poverty. This mindset reveals how the colonial trope of white men as saviors still lingers in many men's psyches.[25] With their financial advantages, American men could access younger women who were willing to accept larger age gaps than what is common in the West or other tour locations like Ukraine and Colombia. In Davao, it was common to see couples with age gaps of twenty to forty years. While relationships between much older foreign men and younger Filipino women are normalized and socially acceptable, relationships between Filipino men and women tend to have smaller age gaps, usually between five and ten years.

Caleb, an affiliate marketer who lived as an expatriate in the Philippines for two years, often remarked that any "nerdy" man could find an attractive Filipino woman to date. Many men I met on tour in the Philippines had previously attended tours in Colombia and Ukraine without success, particularly when it came to finding a wife who would accept an age gap of more than ten to fifteen years. The accessibility of women's various forms of labor in the Philippines, combined with their youth, English skills, and conservative values, has made the country a prime destination for marriage within the international dating industry. Men felt successful on romance tours, as they were able to extract young women's aesthetic, reproductive, intimate, and emotional labor.

6

Marriage

Happily Ever After?

The ultimate goal of romance tourism and the international dating industry is to find a wife. When discussing my research, the most common question I receive is, "How successful are the men in finding a wife?" Historically, wives have provided intimate, reproductive, emotional, and aesthetic labor to benefit their husbands, and this trend continues today, even as women challenge some expectations regarding marriage and work outside the home.[1] Gender inequalities remain deeply rooted in heteronormative systems, as men gain masculinity capital by accessing women's various forms of labor and femininity capital.

Men in this industry approach intimate relationships with a market-based, neoliberal mindset. They hire large international dating agencies or boutique matchmakers to help them access women's labor in countries they view as more traditional in gender norms. These men believe women in these countries will be impressed by their relative affluence as Western or American men. Geographer Matthew Hayes argues that migrants from the Global North who move to the Global South are engaging in a form of global arbitrage, since they are moving to spaces with lower costs of living with their relative affluence.[2] Similarly, some men in my study engage in global intimate arbitrage, using their relative affluence to impress younger and more beautiful women than they believe are accessible to them in the United States.

As feminists and queer theorists have shown, marriage tends to benefit men more than women, as men directly gain from women's various forms of labor.[3] Men's entitlement to women's labor, such as aesthetic, emotional, reproductive, and sexual, drives their search for potential wives abroad. Convinced by red pill ideology and certain media that traditional families in the West are under attack, men attend romance tours seeking the feminine labor they believe is missing in Western society. They often criticize Western women for being too independent, demanding, and career-oriented, while praising women in the Global South as more traditional and feminine. However, they also sometimes label non-Western women as potential gold diggers, contradicting their earlier praises of non-Western women as different from Western women.

Men from the West often believe they have an economic advantage over women outside the West, imagining these women as poor and desperate to date any man with a decent job. The majority of men I interviewed felt invisible and alone in their home countries, often bitter from difficult marriages. They expressed similar complaints about Western women, deeming them selfish for not wanting to perform traditional femininity. Consequently, these men devalue Western women while romanticizing women in the Global South as untainted by feminism and still willing to perform femininity's traditional labor.

The men I met on tour felt more empowered and masculine in non-Western geographic spaces, often noting they had more choices abroad. They described feeling desired and noticed, while in the United States, they felt invisible to women. Younger women's aesthetic labor was more accessible to them outside the West. They frequently commented that women in Ukraine, Colombia, and the Philippines were thinner, prettier, and dressed more femininely than their Western counterparts. They also accessed women's intimate and emotional labor through dating during the tour and by writing to women on the website. Countries outside the West appear to these men as new intimate frontiers where they can use their affluence to access and extract women's various forms of labor and femininity capital.

These men define their masculinity through their access to women's labor, which becomes more valuable when it generates femininity capital. Women who dress femininely, wearing high heels and dresses, are considered more valuable in defining men's heteromasculinity. In previous publications, I have shown that heterosexual men gain a masculinity boost from younger and more conventionally attractive women, viewing women's bodies, aesthetic labor, and femininity capital as a "trophy" that validates them among other men and elevates their status in the hierarchy of straight men.[4] Beyond aesthetic labor, men desire women who will enhance their masculinity by performing reproductive labor at home, such as cooking, cleaning, and child-rearing. They also seek emotional labor, moral support, intimate conversations, and sexual labor to feel masculine.

I refer back to Kate Manne's idea of misogyny as a system that polices and enforces asymmetric social roles between men and women to extract more labor and resources from women.[5] The men in my study described the rise of feminist ideals as hindering their access to women's various forms of labor and femininity capital, as Western women no longer happily serve in asymmetric social roles and expect more equal treatment. Anthony Giddens's definition of a "pure" relationship suggests that heterosexual relationships in Western societies are moving toward more equality with the advent of women's birth control and what he calls "plastic sexuality."[6] However, many men resist the idea of egalitarian relationships. As Jane Ward points out, men are having a difficult time transitioning from viewing women as their property to viewing them as their equals, which is causing a great deal of strain in heterosexual relationships.[7]

Numerous media sources and scholars consider the men in my study extremely misogynistic because they seek unequal, "traditional" heterosexual relationships and are seeking to find them with women in poorer countries. Based on Western men's geographic, economic, and gendered positions, people assume that the men participating in romance tours exploit economically disadvantaged women. However, all heteromasculinity is based on accessing women's labor and femininity capital; these men are not unusual in their desire for a trophy wife who performs most of the labor at home. For example, data from OkCupid, an online free domestic dating site in the United States, shows that men of every age group and racial group consistently rate women in their twenties as the most attractive on the website, demonstrating men's preferences for a youthful trophy wife in the aggregate.[8] Femininity is associated with youth and beauty, and women who conform to conventional norms of white femininity (thin and lighter-skinned) are more valued in the dating marketplace. For example, men are willing to accept darker-skinned women in the Philippines and Colombia but do not want women who are Black. The company I followed does not provide tours in any African countries, despite a growing sex and romance tourism industry there.[9]

Despite their assumptions, men's relative affluence did not necessarily translate into successful marriages or long-term relationships. During my time observing tours, most men I met did not end up getting married. However, some couples did marry, and this chapter briefly examines the marital negotiations surrounding women's labor and femininity capital once women migrate as wives. As noted in previous chapters, most of these couples are an American man and a Filipino woman.

Marital Negotiations

The couples I followed from the Philippines tours have largely experienced long-term success, despite many people's perception that these marriages are simply for green cards. Even after a decade, most of the couples I follow who got married are still together, and many have children. The couples I track on social media and through follow-up interviews are geographically dispersed. For example, Belinda and Charles are still married and living in Hawaii with their two young children. Before becoming a mother, Belinda worked in hospitality at a large hotel in Hawaii. Her transition to life in Hawaii was relatively smooth, as many Filipinos live on the island, allowing her to find a community. Before COVID, Belinda and Charles were attempting to start their own adventure tour company, taking Americans to explore the Philippines. Both are athletic and active and want to introduce people to the natural wonders of the Philippines. For now, however, Belinda stays at home, focusing on raising their two daughters.

Belinda's best friend, Madeline, married a significantly older man. Despite their twenty-year age gap, she was determined to have children. Madeline got engaged at thirty-one, while her husband was in his early fifties. They currently live in West Virginia, where Madeline is a stay-at-home mother. While she does not work, she is attending a local university. Madeline also had a relatively smooth transition to the United States, as her husband's adult children and extended family accepted her. Before migrating, Madeline was focused on having children as soon as possible, hoping for a large family. Now, she has two sons and a daughter, ranging from two to six years old, and she is actively involved in the local Filipino community in West Virginia.

During the tour in the Philippines, Riley and I spent time with Jayson, a man in his late forties who showed interest in potentially dating Riley. We all went to a bar together, and it became clear that Riley had no romantic interest in him. Later in the tour, Jayson met another woman, Jane, who was in her early thirties and had a young son from a previous relationship. They got engaged by the end of the tour, and Jane moved to Arizona with her son, whom Jayson formally adopted. Jane attended nursing school full time and began modeling and working out regularly. Jayson bought her breast implants, cars, and numerous expensive purses. While Jane consistently told me she was happy in Arizona and school, she often fought with Jayson, feeling insecure and jealous of his intentions toward potential other women.

While at a local bar in Davao with Riley, I met an older retired American man who eagerly approached me upon hearing my American accent. During my time in Davao, I was frequently asked why I was there, as not many white American women travel there. Jim, the man I met, asked me the same question. When I explained my research project, he gave me the contact information for a young American man, Lenny, married to a young Filipino woman who was still living in Davao. I contacted Lenny, and we met as a group with his wife and young child at the local mall. Lenny was much younger than the typical men on tour, especially those looking to settle down, get married, and have children. When I asked why such a young man decided to get married in the Philippines, Lenny laughed and explained, "My mom saw me partying hard, not going anywhere positive or good. She pushed me to come to the Philippines, believe it or not, and to find a good woman who was willing to settle down and have a family. I was only eighteen, but I was already a wild child, and my mom thought a wife would help me calm down, chill out." I was also surprised that Lenny had chosen to stay in the Philippines instead of returning to the United States for the past three years.

Lenny explained that, initially, he was working online, making good money, and living comfortably in the Philippines with a nice apartment in a gated community. However, by the time of our interview three years later, he and his family had had to move multiple times, each time downgrading their lifestyle. Lenny's online job became less lucrative, and each new apartment had fewer amenities. By the time we spoke, they were living like locals, without air conditioning or reliable electricity.

Throughout the interview, Lenny's wife, Glenda, expressed frustration that he still wanted to go out drinking and partying, despite raising a young child. She was tired and wanted him to focus more on being a good father. Given their lower standard of living and Glenda's desire for Lenny to calm down, they decided to return to the United States and start over in Las Vegas, with help from Lenny's mother. Although Lenny was nervous about moving back to Vegas, as he had not fully calmed down from marriage and fatherhood, he felt it was the right decision to provide for his family. "I guess it's time to go back. I can't make real money online out here anymore, and I need to provide a better life for my family," he said. Lenny was confident that more opportunities to earn money were still available in the United States, and his wife believed their daughter would have better educational opportunities there.

Darren and Alma remain happily married in Tennessee, where Darren formally adopted Alma's young daughter, who is active in martial arts. A few years into her transition to life in the United States, Alma and I had lunch together. She expressed her happiness at being in a more financially stable position, which allowed her to spend more time with her daughter. Alma explained that if she had not met Darren when she did, she would have returned to Saudi Arabia to work as a nurse to support her parents and daughter. She consistently praised Halia's agency for allowing her to meet a man who accepted both her and her child. Alma still remits money to her parents in the Philippines and plans to continue supporting them for the rest of their lives.

Veronica, who worked at the local office and had a profile on the website, ended up messaging a man she was attracted to after her failed date with Leon. He visited her shortly after I left the Philippines in 2012. They hit it off immediately, even though he was relatively shy. By the end of his trip, Scott had met Veronica's family and proposed to her. Scott, a decade older than Veronica, was considered a blessing by her, as he was both good-looking and hardworking. Her K-1 visa was processed quickly, and she moved with Scott to a rural town in Oregon. During her first few years in the United States, Veronica became quite depressed. Despite her strict upbringing as a Jehovah's Witness, she had a lot of freedom in Davao. She worked, used public transport, and spent time with friends. In Oregon, however, she felt completely isolated, unable to drive or leave her house except when Scott took her out.

While in the United States, Veronica's father inherited a farm on the island of Bohol, and Scott agreed to let her move home to plan his retirement there. He sold his home in Oregon to purchase a plot of farmland near Veronica's family land in Bohol. Veronica said, "Scott hates Davao but loves Bohol. He wants the quiet, peaceful island life, and the city life is too busy for him. I think it's kind of boring compared to my life in Davao." They got scammed on the first piece of land they tried to buy but eventually purchased a farm. However, Scott decided they did not have enough savings and that he should work a few more years to add to their funds. He left the Philippines just as COVID started, which separated the couple for two years. While waiting for Scott to return, Veronica opened a small sari-sari store on her father's land to keep herself occupied.[10]

In addition to these couples, many others remain together in the United States and Australia. Based on my limited data, Filipino women seem more likely to marry and stay married to foreign men. On the other hand, the majority of couples I met from Ukraine and Colombia ended up divorcing. For instance, I met Alexa, a Ukrainian woman who worked in the Kyiv AFA office, married an Asian American man, and migrated to Southern California. At the time we met, Alexa had been married to her husband for eight years but was very unhappy with how her marriage was going. Her husband, Peter, had children from a previous marriage, and his ex-wife did not approve of his new marriage. Alexa would complain, "He lets his kids do whatever they want. They do not respect me or really him. They want to smoke pot and just hang out playing video games. They never listen to me when I ask them to help out around the house." In addition to issues with her stepchildren, Alexa lived in a relatively isolated area, and her husband often was emotionally abusive.

Alexa would complain to me that whenever she would argue with her husband, he would turn something off in her car or suspend her credit cards so she could not leave. She would complain that she felt trapped in this isolated mountain town and often would tell me that she regretted leaving Kyiv, as life seemed to be a struggle: "You know, everyone in Ukraine thinks that money just grows on trees here. They don't understand that good jobs are hard to find, and that life is so expensive." As she contemplated leaving her husband, Alexa's main worry focused on being able to financially sustain herself on her relatively low pay working as an administrative office employee. Five years ago, she finally decided to commit to starting her life over and proceeded to divorce her husband. He kept the house and she moved to a small apartment he owned in a more urban environment than the small mountain town where they lived as a couple. Alexa was struggling financially, as the main type of work she could find was largely as an administrative assistant, which did not pay enough for her to live very comfortably. Leaving her husband was very difficult, as she was in her mid-thirties and felt like he took her youth and her opportunity to have children. However, three years ago her choice seemed to be the best one she could have made, as her husband died from injecting himself with homemade Botox that he was selling.

During my second trip to Medellín in 2016, Karina, the former translator and local AFA employee, had switched jobs to work in customer service for an American-based company. She excitedly told me she had arranged an interview with her colleague, Jimmy, who had moved to Colombia with his wife but was recently divorced. When I met Jimmy, he was working in the same low-end position as Karina, even though he was a native English speaker. We met after work, and I began interviewing him over some local beers. Jimmy explained, "I'm originally from Ohio and came to Medellín five years ago on a tour with AFA. I met my wife on that tour, got engaged six months later, and she moved to my home in Ohio." Jimmy owned a home in Ohio and was working a relatively low-paying job when his wife, Danisa, arrived in the United States. Danisa worked as a hairstylist for a few years, but they lived modestly overall.

When Danisa's grandfather died, they had the opportunity to buy his home in Bello, a large working-class suburb north of Medellín. However, they could not afford to purchase her family home without selling their home in Ohio. Jimmy and Danisa decided it would be more advantageous to move back to Colombia, as they were not doing well financially in the United States, and they could buy her family's home for relatively little. Jimmy was happy with the move to Medellín, especially since their new home was next door to Danisa's child-hood home. However, once they settled in Colombia, Jimmy noticed a shift in their relationship. "Once we came back to Colombia, Danisa felt instantly more comfortable. She was less interested in spending time with me, since now she had all of her friends and family around." Jimmy felt increasingly isolated, working long hours with little free time and no social connections outside of work. Meanwhile, Danisa became more integrated into her family's lives.

Two years after their move, Jimmy explained that their relationship fell apart. "I was working a ton, and she was just with her family all the time. She never wanted to spend time with me when I was actually home. I felt so alone." Eventually, Danisa told Jimmy she wanted a divorce and planned to keep the house, as it was her family home. Jimmy was devastated and unsure whether to return to the United States as a single man or try to build a new life in Colombia. Since he already had a job in Colombia, he decided to stay and found his own apartment in Bello. "The apartment is small, but I don't need much space now that I'm by myself. It ain't too bad. My job pays okay, and life is just cheap and easy here. The U.S. is so much stress." Despite the divorce, Jimmy felt his chances of finding a new rela-tionship were better if he stayed in Colombia. "Yeah, I go up to AFA and have them arrange dates for me now and again, but I still haven't met anyone I'm seriously into." Even though his marriage ended in divorce, Jimmy chose to continue living in Colombia rather than return to the United States and start over again.

Rates of Success

For men involved in the romance tour industry, marriage is the ultimate goal. However, most men do not achieve success in finding a long-term relationship, let alone marriage. The majority choose to remain "keyboard Romeos," maintaining fantasy correspondence-based relationships rather than meeting the women in person. According to AFA statistics, 90 percent of men choose to stay online, making them more susceptible to correspondence-based scams. To counter this, smaller boutique matchmakers have shifted away from the correspondence model, encouraging men to travel overseas and meet the women in person. Men who are willing to travel abroad tend to be more serious and dedicated to finding a potential wife than most men on international dating websites. Reputable agencies like AFA advise men not to send money to women they have not met in person to avoid falling victim to online love scams.

As previously mentioned, most men who do get married end up with Filipino women. Men often struggle to find meaningful relationships in other tour locations, particularly in Ukraine. Large tour companies like AFA generally lack accurate data on the number of couples who end up marrying, as many men choose not to self-report the successes or failures of their relationships. Natali, however, kept detailed records of her successful couples, as her matchmaking services focused on creating intimate bonds with her clients. The median age of men who successfully married was fifty-two, which was close to the median age of her entire database. She found that men who committed to visiting as much as possible had the best chances of cultivating a lasting relationship. This naturally requires men to have the time and resources to travel to Ukraine frequently to establish a real connection and to maintain it.

The quick engagements I witnessed in the Philippines during the romance tour were unusual in Colombia and Ukraine. The one engagement I observed in Ukraine involved a man in his late fifties and a woman in her early forties. He opted for more realistic, age-appropriate dating in Ukraine. Most men in his age group, however, chose not to date women in their forties, focusing instead on much younger women in their twenties and thirties. While many men cited their desire for younger women as based on their wish to have children, large age gaps in Ukraine and Colombia were less likely to succeed or be taken seriously by women. For this reason, John from AFA always encouraged men seeking much younger women to attend tours in the Philippines, where it is more socially acceptable for women to date much older foreign men.

Several men discussed moving to one of these three countries upon retirement, and some did retire with their wives. This challenges the narrative that these relationships are solely about women migrating as brides to places like the United States. The men who chose to retire in places like the Philippines engaged in the geographic arbitrage highlighted by geographer Mike Hawkins in his discussion of U.S. retirement migrants in the Philippines.[11] These men often sell all their major assets to afford a better life abroad on their retirement pensions or Social Security payments. Jimmy in Medellín and Lenny in the Philippines defied the norm by migrating before retirement age and attempting to work and live in the Global South on local salaries. Many men, particularly veterans, viewed the Philippines as an ideal retirement location due to the numerous services available through Veterans Affairs there.

Future of the Industry

During my time at industry conferences, the international dating sector rebranded itself as the Premium International Dating (PID) market, attempting to dissociate from negative stereotypes that equate "mail order brides" with human trafficking. Before 2020, the industry in Ukraine was shifting toward more personalized matchmaking services, similar to those offered by Natali and Alex through their small boutique agencies. While romance tours remained popular, the largest online international dating company, AnastasiaDate, stopped offering tours and instead promoted live and video chat options. As the industry's largest company shifted to more online content, other companies followed suit, and romance tours largely ended during the COVID-19 pandemic.

The COVID-19 pandemic posed new challenges for introduction agencies that provided in-person services, such as matchmaking and tours. The industry's focus returned to its online format as many men, confined to their homes, sought connections with women abroad, even if only through chat or email correspondence. The pandemic also delayed K-1 fiancé visa processing timelines, forcing many couples to separate for months, if not years. As embassies and consulates closed to prevent the spread of COVID, a significant backlog of visa applications developed. Although the pandemic has subsided and international travel has resumed, companies like AFA have reduced the number of tours they offer. For instance, AFA offered four tours annually in Medellín in 2012, but now only offers two. Beyond the shift to online spaces, COVID also ended the international dating conferences organized by IDATE, a company that was devoted to gathering various companies within the dating industry to conference together, as large gatherings became impractical.

The most significant recent development impacting the industry has been the war in Ukraine. In February 2022, Russia invaded Ukraine, dramatically altering the landscape of the international dating industry, particularly for local matchmakers and romance tour providers based in Ukraine. While both AFA and Mark Davis's Dream Connections company operate in other countries, Ukraine was always their primary tour destination. AFA has suspended tours to Ukraine, as the ongoing war makes the country unsafe for tourism, and Dream Connections has completely shut down its website. Mark Davis has left the international dating industry altogether and now promotes himself as a masculinity coach. Numerous small matchmakers have been displaced; Alex moved back to his home country of Portugal, while others in the industry relocated to Bulgaria, Germany, and the UK. Many smaller matchmakers are struggling to sustain their businesses, as the war has halted most men's travel plans. Some matchmakers have moved their meetings to Zoom or other video call platforms, as more women seek partners abroad due to the war.

Around 8 million refugees have left Ukraine, with many relocating to various European Union countries. The majority of refugees are women and children, as men eligible for military recruitment are not legally allowed to leave the country. While most refugees are permitted to live abroad, many struggle to find legal employment in their host countries for extended periods, if ever. I have observed matchmakers frequently moving between countries, such as a matchmaker from Odesa who fled to Bulgaria, returned to Odesa, attempted to move to Canada, and ultimately returned to Bulgaria. She continues to run her matchmaking business online from Bulgaria, encouraging couples to meet in neutral countries like Türkiye. Another high-end boutique matchmaker relocated to Germany and continues to run her matchmaking business online, including introductions and recruiting women. She argues on her YouTube channel that COVID prepared matchmakers to work remotely and that her boutique agency can still successfully match couples online.

As the war continues, the situation grows increasingly complex for many matchmakers. Some have become refugees, while others choose to remain in Ukraine, but the industry has experienced a significant slowdown. The cottage matchmaking industry has been hit even harder, as their business model relies heavily on in-person interactions. Small boutique matchmaking agencies offer various personal services that can adapt to remote work, but some men are unwilling to pay the higher fees matchmakers charge for remote services. With the war's duration uncertain, most tour providers in Ukraine remain hopeful that the conflict will end soon. However, the nature of the industry in Ukraine will have dramatically shifted, as many Ukrainian women are now able to stay in Western countries as refugees and no longer need to marry for access to legal residence.

ACKNOWLEDGMENTS

I begin by acknowledging the unwavering support from both of my parents, Csilla and Attila Meszaros. I would like to thank Alison Higgins, Rebecca Bertler, Justin Manu, Wilfredo Martinez, Sarah Julius, Heather Manring, Minakshi De Almeida, Melissa Howe, Meghan Ruder Findley, Isis Darios, and Emily Feistel for their unwavering friendship throughout the decades. I could not imagine completing this project without these deep and affirming relationships.

In terms of early development of this project, I would like to extend a heartfelt thank you to my dissertation advisor Vrushali Patil, who helped guide me through the dissertation process with grace. I am also grateful to the rest of my dissertation committee for their thoughtful feedback and encouragement: Percy Hintzen, Caroline Faria, Jean Rahier, and Alexandra Cornelius. After graduating, I am eternally indebted to Rhacel Salazar Parreñas for her mentorship and guidance with expanding this project and her invaluable feedback in transforming my dissertation into this book. I would also like to thank Haiyi Liu, Maria Cecilia Hwang, Carolyn Choi, Minwoo Jung, and Emmanuel David for their feedback and collaboration throughout the years.

I am grateful to have participated in writing groups at Texas A&M Commerce that provided me with amazing insights from scholars both in my discipline and beyond it. I want to extend my gratitude to Zachary Palmer, Kelin Loe, Rebecca Rowe, and Veronica Duran for their extensive comments and insightful feedback on various drafts of this manuscript. I have also enjoyed numerous intellectual conversations about this project with dear friends and colleagues, including Mamyrah Douge-Prosper, Brandon Andrew Robinson, Samantha Bowden, Kimiko Haru Tanita, Dominika Bukalova, Nicole Farris, and Vlad Khaykin, to whom I am also indebted for their insights and ideas. I am particularly thankful to Mark Goldstone for reading the entire manuscript and providing very thoughtful feedback.

I met some amazing people in the field who helped me navigate various localities and make my time in the field much more enjoyable. In Colombia, Katherine Orrego Jimenez and Jolie Belinsky made my time so memorable; we have an unimaginable bond that transcends borders. In Colombia, I would also like to thank Estefanía Vergara and David Castro for their support and help. In

Ukraine, I would like to thank Vitaly Gadzhiev and Iryna Khomenko for showing me around Kyiv and collaborating with my students to spread the word about the war in Ukraine. I would also like to thank Konstantin Lytvyn and Julia Prysada for showing me around Kyiv and Odesa and opening their home to me. In the Philippines, I would like to thank Robbie Jean Soco for showing me around Davao and Vivian Janolo for opening her home to me in Bohol . I would also like to thank Helen.

This project would not exist without the access that the industry provided me. For this reason, I need to extend a special thank you to John Adams, for agreeing to allow me access to any romance tour that A Foreign Affair provided, and for supporting my research throughout the years. I would also like to thank Natali Koval for providing me with access to her matchmaking office and for supporting scientific endeavors surrounding the industry. I would like to thank Alex Pinto, Elena Vygnanyuk, Mark Brooks, and Mark Davis for their extensive help in understanding the industry.

The project would also not exist without the participation of men and women whom I met during my fieldwork and years spent following the industry. I am forever indebted to all of them for sharing their personal lives and love stories with me, allowing me to be part of their lives for years. Finally, I want to acknowledge my two angels, Michiko Haru Tanita and Victoria J. Bertics, for inspiring me to keep going and finish this project.

NOTES

INTRODUCTION: MASCULINITY AS ACCESS TO WOMEN'S LABOR

1. I recognize the term "Western" is loaded with Orientalist and colonial undertones (please see Edward Said's 1978 book *Orientalism*, published by Vintage Books, and numerous other postcolonial and transnational feminist scholars, such as Chandra Mohanty) but I am using the terminology employed by the industry and the men I interviewed participating.

2. All participants' names are changed in order to protect their privacy, except for those industry participants who wanted their identity and company to be named. I want to point out that Nikola chose his pseudonym as a big fan of Nikola Tesla.

3. All unsourced material quoted in this book is from personal interviews I conducted from 2011 to 2023.

4. "The manosphere" is an umbrella term that describes an online-based community that includes groups such as involuntary celibates, pick up artists, MGTOW, and men's rights activists. These groups generally identify as "red pilled," meaning they believe the world is misandric and that men are disadvantaged within intimate relationships in the Western world. In this worldview, intimacy and attractiveness are all quantified and thought of in an economic sense. Each community differs in how they address their solutions to dealing with women. Please refer to my article in the journal *About Gender* for more information, Julia Meszaros, "The Manosphere: International Dating and the Crisis of Access," *AG About Gender-International Journal of Gender Studies* 10, no. 19 (2021): 199–223.

5. Involuntary celibates believe they can never find a woman willing to have sex with them, believing that only the top 20 percent of attractive men are able to secure sex with women, at least the extremely attractive women these men are attracted to. MGTOW instead preach you can have sex with women but to treat them as sex workers and never to marry them or get emotionally involved. Thus, while Nikola self-identified as MGTOW, he thought marrying a woman from Eastern Europe would avoid the issues with marriage in the United States.

6. Meszaros, "The Manosphere, International Dating and the Crisis of Access."

7. Beth Montemurro, *Getting It, Having It, Keeping It Up: Straight Men's Sexuality in Public and Private* (New Brunswick, NJ: Rutgers University Press, 2021).

8. Trad-con means traditional-conservatism.

9. Viviana Zelizer, *The Purchase of Intimacy* (Princeton, NJ: Princeton University Press, 2005).

10. Candace West and Don H. Zimmerman, "Doing Gender," *Gender & Society* 1, no. 2 (1987): 125–151.

11. Judith Butler, *Gender Trouble: Feminism and the Subversion of Identity* (New York: Routledge, 2011).

12. Catherine Hakim, *Erotic Capital: The Power of Attraction in the Boardroom and the Bedroom* (New York: Basic Books, 2011); John Levi Martin and Matt George, "Theories of Sexual Stratification: Toward an Analytics of the Sexual Field and a Theory of Sexual Capital," *Sociological Theory* 24, no. 2 (2006): 107–132.

13. Hakim, *Erotic Capital*.

14. Pierre Bourdieu, *Distinction: A Social Critique of the Judgment of Taste* (Cambridge, MA: Harvard University Press, 1984); Robert D. Putnam, *Bowling Alone: The Collapse and Revival of American Community* (New York: Simon and Schuster, 2000); David Throsby, "Cultural Capital," *Journal of Cultural Economics* 23 (1999): 3–12.

15. Hakim, *Erotic Capital*.

16. Adam Isaiah Green, "'Erotic Capital' and the Power of Desirability: Why 'Honey Money' is a Bad Collective Strategy for Remedying Gender Inequality," *Sexualities* 16, no. 1–2 (2013): 137–158; Alicia Valdés Lucas, "Can Erotic Capital Subvert Masculine Economy? Aesthetic Work and the Post-Feminist Approach to Economics/¿Puede el Capital Erótico Subvertir la Economía Masculina? Aesthetic Work y el Enfoque Postfeminista Hacia la Economía," *RECERCA. Revista de Pensament i Anàlisi* 24, no. 2 (2019): 87–108.

17. Dana Kaplan and Eva Illouz, *What is Sexual Capital?* (New York: Wiley, 2022).

18. Erin Rodgers (@ErinMRodgers), "I want the term 'gold digger' to include dudes who look for a woman who will do tons of emotional labour for them," Twitter (now X), June 1, 2016, https://x.com/ErinMRodgers/status/738195765030313985, quoted in Melanie Hamlett, "Men Have No Friends and Women Bear the Burden," *Harper's Bazaar*, May 2, 2019, https://www.harpersbazaar.com/culture/features/a27259689/toxic-masculinity-male-friendships-emotional-labor-men-rely-on-women/; Jane Ward, *The Tragedy of Heterosexuality* (New York: New York University Press, 2022).

19. Belinda Luscombe, "Men Want to Remarry; Women are 'Meh'," *Time Magazine*, November 14, 2014, https://time.com/3584827/pew-marriage-divorce-remarriage/; Libby Richards, Melissa Franks, Rosie Shrout, and the Conversation, "Married Men Are Healthier than Everyone Else. Here's Why They Get the Best End of the Deal," *Fortune*, January 13, 2023, https://fortune.com/2023/01/13/why-are-married-men-healthier-on-average-women-gender-research/.

20. Michele Weiner-Davis, "The Walkaway Wife Syndrome," *Psychology Today*, March 30, 2008, https://www.psychologytoday.com/us/blog/divorce-busting/200803/the-walkaway-wife-syndrome.

21. Silvia Federici, "Marx and Feminism," *TripleC: Communication, Capitalism & Critique. Open Access Journal for a Global Sustainable Information Society* 16, no. 2 (2018): 468–475; Michele Barrett, *Women's Oppression Today: The Marxist/Feminist Encounter* (New York: Verso Books, 2014).

22. Evelyn Nakano Glenn, "From Servitude to Service Work: Historical Continuities in the Racial Division of Paid Reproductive Labor," *Signs: Journal of Women in Culture and Society* 18, no. 1 (1992): 1–43.

23. Evelyn Nakano Glenn, *Unequal Freedom: How Race and Gender Shaped American Citizenship and Labor* (Cambridge, MA: Harvard University Press, 2004).

24. Nakano Glenn, "From Servitude to Service Work"; Rhacel Parreñas, *Servants of Globalization: Migration and Domestic Work* (Stanford, CA: Stanford University Press, 2015);

Nicola Yeates, *Globalizing Care Economies and Migrant Workers: Explorations in Global Care Chains* (Basingstoke, UK: Palgrave Macmillan, 2009).

25. Arlie Hochschild, *The Managed Heart: Commercialization of Human Feeling* (Berkeley: University of California Press, 1983).

26. Ashley Mears, *Very Important People: Status and Beauty in the Global Party Circuit* (Princeton, NJ: Princeton University Press, 2011).

27. Samantha Kwan and Mary Nell Trautner, "Beauty Work: Individual and Institutional Rewards, the Reproduction of Gender, and Questions of Agency," *Sociology Compass* 3, no. 1 (2009): 49–71.

28. Megan Rivers-Moore, *Gringo Gulch: Sex, Tourism, and Social Mobility in Costa Rica* (Chicago: University of Chicago Press, 2016).

29. Megan Rivers-Moore, "Affective Sex: Beauty, Race and Nation in the Sex Industry," *Feminist Theory* 14, no. 2 (2013): 153–169.

30. Eileen Boris and Rhacel Salazar Parreñas, eds., *Intimate Labors: Cultures, Technologies, and the Politics of Care* (Stanford, CA: Stanford University Press, 2010), 1–12.

31. Boris and Parreñas, *Intimate Labors.*

32. Eileen Boris, Stephanie Gilmore, and Rhacel Parrenas, "Sexual Labors: Interdisciplinary Perspectives Toward Sex as Work," *Sexualities* 13, no. 2 (2010): 131–137.

33. Boris and Parreñas, *Intimate Labors.*

34. Rhacel Salazar Parreñas, Hung Cam Thai, and Rachel Silvey, "Guest Editors' Introduction—Intimate Industries: Restructuring (Im)Material Labor in Asia," *Positions: Asia Critique* 24, no.1 (2016): 1–15, Project MUSE.

35. Jane Ward, "Gender Labor," in *Intimate Labors: Cultures, Technologies, and the Politics of Care*, ed. Eileen Boris and Rhacel Salazar Parreñas (Stanford, CA: Stanford University Press, 2010): 78–93.

36. Carla A. Pfeffer, "'Women's Work?' Women Partners of Transgender Men Doing Housework and Emotion Work," *Journal of Marriage and Family* 72, no.1 (2010): 165–183; Ward, "Gender Labor," 78.

37. Brandon Andrew Robinson, "Transamorous Misogyny: Masculinity, Heterosexuality, and Cis Men's Sexist Desires for Trans Women," *Men and Masculinities* 26, no. 3 (2023): 356–375, https://doi.org/10.1177/1097184X221148208.

38. Marc Goni, "Assortative Matching at the Top of the Distribution: Evidence from the World's Most Exclusive Marriage Market," *American Economic Journal: Applied Economics* 14, no. 3 (2022): 445–487.

39. Stephen Whyte, Robert C. Brooks, and Benno Torgler, "Sexual Economic Theory & the Human Mating Market," *Applied Economics* 51, no. 57 (2019): 6100–6112.

40. Roy F. Baumeister and Kathleen D. Vohs, "Sexual Economics: Sex as Female Resource for Social Exchange in Heterosexual Interactions," *Personality and Social Psychology Review* 8, no. 4 (2004): 339–363.

41. Stephanie Coontz, *Marriage, a History: How Love Conquered Marriage* (New York: Penguin Books, 2006); Carole Pateman, "Sexual Contract," in *The Wiley Blackwell Encyclopedia of Gender and Sexuality Studies*, ed. Nancy A. Naples (Hoboken, NJ: Wiley Blackwell, 2016), 1–3; Gayle S. Rubin, "Thinking Sex: Notes for a Radical Theory of the Politics of Sexuality," *Culture, Society and Sexuality A Reader* (New York: Routledge, 2002), 143–178.

42. Adrienne Rich, "Compulsory Heterosexuality and Lesbian Existence," *Signs: Journal of Women in Culture and Society* 5, no. 4 (1980): 631–660.

43. Friedrich Engels, *The Origin of the Family, Private Property and the State* (New York: Verso Books, 1972).

44. Engels, *The Origin of the Family.*

45. Nakano Glenn, "From Servitude to Service Work."

46. Nakano Glenn, "From Servitude to Service Work"; Mignon Duffy, "Doing the Dirty Work: Gender, Race, and Reproductive Labor in Historical Perspective," *Gender & Society* 21, no. 3 (2007): 313–336.

47. Yeates, *Globalizing Care Economies and Migrant Workers*; Parreñas, *Servants of Globalization*; Lisa Dodson and Rebekah M. Zincavage, "'It's like a Family': Caring Labor, Exploitation, and Race in Nursing Homes," *Gender & Society* 21, no. 6 (2007): 905–928.

48. Patricia Hill Collins, *Black Feminist Thought: Knowledge, Consciousness, and the Politics of Empowerment* (New York: Routledge Press, 2022).

49. Da'Shaun L. Harrison, *Belly of the Beast: The Politics of Anti-Fatness as Anti-Blackness* (Berkeley, CA: North Atlantic Books, 2021).

50. Kamala Kempadoo, "Introduction: Globalizing Sex Workers Rights," in *Global Sex Workers* (New York: Routledge, 2018), 1–28.

51. Ward, *The Tragedy of Heterosexuality.*

52. Ward, *The Tragedy of Heterosexuality*, 25.

53. Kate Manne, *Down Girl: The Logic of Misogyny* (Oxford: Oxford University Press, 2017).

54. Manne, *Down Girl.*

55. Rachel O'Neill, *Seduction: Men, Masculinity and Mediated Intimacy* (New York: Wiley, 2018); Ward, *The Tragedy of Heterosexuality.*

56. Matthew Hayes, "'We Gained a Lot over What We Would Have Had': The Geographic Arbitrage of North American Lifestyle Migrants to Cuenca, Ecuador," *Journal of Ethnic and Migration Studies* 40, no. 12 (2014): 1953–1971.

57. Eva Illouz, *Consuming the Romantic Utopia: Love and the Cultural Contradictions of Capitalism* (Berkeley: University of California Press, 1997); Mark B. Padilla, Jennifer S. Hirsch, Miguel Munoz-Laboy, Robert E. Sember, and Richard G. Parker, "Love and Globalization," *Transformations of Intimacy in the Contemporary World* (Nashville: Vanderbilt University Press, 2007).

58. Zelizer, *The Purchase of Intimacy.*

59. Coontz, *Marriage, a History.*

60. Lauren Berlant, *Cruel Optimism* (Durham, NC: Duke University Press, 2020), 85.

61. O'Neill, *Seduction.*

62. Vrushali Patil, *Webbed Connectivities: The Imperial Sociology of Sex, Gender and Sexuality* (Minneapolis: University of Minnesota Press, 2022).

63. Anna Lowenhaupt Tsing, *Friction: An Ethnography of Global Connection* (Princeton, NJ: Princeton University Press, 2011).

64. Nicole Constable, *Romance on a Global Stage: Pen Pals, Virtual Ethnography, and "Mail Order" Marriages* (Berkeley: University of California Press, 2003); Felicity Amaya Schaeffer, *Love and Empire: Cybermarriage and Citizenship Across the Americas* (New York: New York University Press, 2013); Monica Liu, *Seeking Western Men: Email-Order Brides Under China's Global Rise* (Stanford, CA: Stanford University Press, 2022).

CHAPTER 1 "MAIL ORDER BRIDES," INTERNATIONAL
DATING, AND INTIMATE FRONTIERS

1. Evelyn Nakano Glenn, "From Servitude to Service Work: Historical Continuities in the Racial Division of Paid Reproductive Labor," *Signs: Journal of Women in Culture and Society* 18, no. 1 (1992): 1–43; Mignon Duffy, "Doing the Dirty Work: Gender, Race, and Reproductive Labor in Historical Perspective," *Gender & Society* 21, no. 3 (2007): 313–336; Eileen Boris and Lisa Prugl, *Homeworkers in Global Perspective: Invisible No More* (New York: Routledge, 2016).

2. Ann Laura Stoler, "Tense and Tender Ties: The Politics of Comparison in North American History and (Post) Colonial Studies," in *Haunted by Empire: Geographies of Intimacy in North American History*, ed. A. L. Stoler (Durham, NC: Duke University Press, 2006), 23–67; Evelyn Nakano Glenn, "Settler Colonialism as Structure: A Framework for Comparative Studies of U.S. Race and Gender Formation," *Sociology of Race and Ethnicity* 1, no. 1 (2015): 52–72; Marcia A. Zug, *Buying a Bride: An Engaging History of Mail-Order Matches* (New York: New York University Press, 2016).

3. Greg Matos, "What's Behind the Rise of Lonely, Single Men?" *Psychology Today*, August 9, 2022, https://www.psychologytoday.com/us/blog/the-state-our-unions/202208/whats-behind-the-rise-lonely-single-men.

4. Roland B. Tolentino, "Bodies, Letters, Catalogs: Filipinas in Transnational Space," *Social Text* 48 (1996): 49–76.

5. Ashley Mears, *Very Important People: Status and Beauty in the Global Party Circuit* (Princeton, NJ: Princeton University Press, 2020).

6. Ann Laura Stoler, *Carnal Knowledge and Imperial Power* (Berkeley: University of California Press, 2002); Linda Bryder, "Sex, Race and Colonialism: An Historiographical Review," *The International History Review* 20, no. 4 (1998): 806–822; Anne McClintock, *Imperial Leather: Race, Gender and Sexuality in the Colonial Conquest* (New York: Routledge, 1995).

7. Stoler, "Tense and Tender Ties"; Ann Laura Stoler, "Intimidation of Empire: Predicaments of the Tactile and Unseen," in *Haunted by Empire: Geographies of Intimacy in North American History*, ed. A. L. Stoler (Durham, NC: Duke University Press, 2006), 1–22.

8. Philippa Levine, "Sexuality, Gender and Empire," in *Gender and Empire*, ed. P. Levine (Oxford: Oxford University Press, 2004), 134–155; Ashwini Tambe, *Codes of Misconduct: Regulating Prostitution in Late Colonial Bombay* (Minneapolis: University of Minnesota Press, 2009); Nayan Shah, "Adjudicating Intimacies on U.S. Frontiers," in *Haunted by Empire: Geographies of Intimacy in North American History*, ed. A. L. Stoler (Durham, NC: Duke University Press, 2006), 116–139.

9. Matthew Lange, James Mahoney, and Matthias Vom Hau, "Colonialism and Development: A Comparative Analysis of Spanish and British Colonies," *American Journal of Sociology* 111, no. 5 (2006): 1412–1462.

10. Deena J. Gonzalez, "Malinche Triangulated, Historically Speaking," in *Feminism, Nation and Myth: La Malinche*, ed. R. Romero and A. N. Harris (Houston: Arte Público Press, 2005), 6–12; Sandra Messinger Cypress, "'Mother' Malinche and Allegories of Gender, Ethnicity and National Identity in Mexico," in *Feminism, Nation and Myth: La Malinche*, ed. R. Romero and A. N. Harris (Houston: Arte Público Press, 2005), 14–32.

11. Zug, *Buying a Bride*.

12. Albert L. Hurtado, *Intimate Frontiers: Sex, Gender, and Culture in Old California* (Albuquerque: University of New Mexico Press, 1999), 2.

13. Chris Enss, *Hearts West: True Stories of Mail-Order Brides on the Frontier* (New York: Rowman & Littlefield, 2005).

14. Enss, *Hearts West.*

15. Julia Bettinotti, "Re-Imagining the Gold Rush: Prospectors, Log Cabins and Mail-Order Brides in Contemporary Western Romances," *Northern Review* 19 (1998).

16. Amy Kaplan and Donald E. Pease, *Cultures of United States Imperialism* (Durham, NC: Duke University Press, 1993); Charles J. Weeks, "The New Frontier, the Great Society, and American Imperialism in Oceania," *Pacific Historical Review* 71, no. 1 (2002): 91–125.

17. Ji-Yeon Yuh, *Beyond the Shadow of Camptown: Korean Military Brides in America*, Nation of Nations 25 (New York: New York University Press, 2002).

18. Philip E. Wolgin and Irene Bloemraad, "'Our Gratitude to Our Soldiers:' Military Spouses, Family Re-unification, and Postwar Immigration Reform," *Journal of Interdisciplinary History* 41, no. 1 (2010): 27–60.

19. Maria Cecilia Hwang and Rhacel Salazar Parreñas, "The Gendered Racialization of Asian Women as Villainous Temptresses," *Gender & Society* 35, no. 4 (2021): 567–576.

20. Maxine Yi Hwa Lee, "A Life Preserver for Battered Immigrant Women: The 1990 Amendments to the Immigration Marriage Fraud Amendments," *Buffalo Law Review* 41 (1993): 779.

21. Nicole Constable, "International Marriage Brokers, Cross-Border Marriages and the U.S. Anti-Trafficking Campaign," *Journal of Ethnic and Migration Studies* 38, no. 7 (2012), 1137–1154.

22. Constable, "International Marriage Brokers."

23. Rhacel Salazar Parreñas, Hung Cam Thai, and Rachel Silvey, "Guest Editors' Introduction—Intimate Industries: Restructuring (Im)Material Labor in Asia," *Positions: Asia Critique* 24, no.1 (2016): 1–15, Project MUSE.

24. Deborah Carr, "The Desire to Date and Remarry Among Older Widows and Widowers," *Journal of Marriage and Family* 66 (2004):1051–1068; Lisa Belkin, "The Mail-Order Bride Business," *New York Times*, May 11, 1986, https://www.nytimes.com/1986/05/11/magazine/the-mail-order-bride-business.html.

25. "Interview with AnastasiaDate, Lawrence Cervantes," *Online Personals Watch: IDEA*, 2013, https://www.onlinepersonalswatch.com/news/2013/02/interview-with-anastasiadates-lawrence-cervantes.html.

26. Roland B. Tolentino, "Bodies, Letters, Catalogs: Filipinas in Transnational Space.," *Social Text* 48, (1996): 49–76.

27. Mark Edward Davis, *Mastering the Adventure of International Dating: Real Answers and Straight Talk for Gen Y-ers, Gen X-ers and Boomers to Finding Romance in Eastern Europe, Latin America and Asia* (Las Vegas: MMIX International Dating for Men, Inc., 2009).

28. Kimberly Kay Hoang, "Transnational Gender Vertigo," *Contexts* 12, no. 2 (2013): 22–26.

29. Monica Liu, *Seeking Western Men: Email-Order Brides Under China's Global Rise* (Stanford, CA: Stanford University Press, 2022).

30. Donna M. Hughes, "The Role of 'Marriage Agencies' in the Sexual Exploitation and Trafficking of Women from the Former Soviet Union," *International Review of Victimology* 11, no. 1 (2004): 49–71.

31. Found on the website, ukrainianmatchmakersalliance.com, accessed February 15, 2022.

32. Anthony Giddens, *The Transformation of Intimacy: Sexuality, Love and Eroticism in Modern Societies* (New York: Wiley, 2013).

33. Nicole Constable, *Romance on a Global Stage: Pen Pals, Virtual Ethnography, and "Mail Order" Marriages* (Berkeley: University of California Press, 2003).

34. "Meet Beautiful and Sincere Ukrainian Girl for Marriage," Prime Matchmaking Company, no date, https://prime-match.com/, accessed October 2020.

35. Salazar Parreñas et al., "Guest Editors' Introduction—Intimate Industries."

36. Barbara Ehrenreich and Arlie Russell Hochschild, eds. *Global Woman: Nannies, Maids, and Sex Workers in the New Economy* (New York: Henry Holt, 2002).

CHAPTER 2   FRONTIER MASCULINITY AS EXTRACTING FEMININITY CAPITAL

1. Kate Manne, *Down Girl: The Logic of Misogyny* (New York: Oxford University Press, 2017).

2. Manne, *Down Girl*.

3. Beth Montemurro, *Getting It, Having It, Keeping It Up: Straight Men's Sexuality in Public and Private* (New Brunswick, NJ: Rutgers University Press, 2021).

4. Jane Ward, *The Tragedy of Heterosexuality* (New York: New York University Press, 2022).

5. Ward, *The Tragedy of Heterosexuality*.

6. Julia Meszaros, "American Men and Romance Tourism: Searching for Traditional Trophy Wives as Status Symbols of Masculinity," *Women's Studies Quarterly* 1 (2017): 225–242.

7. Montemurro, *Getting It, Having It, Keeping It Up*.

8. Anthony Giddens, *The Transformation of Intimacy: Sexuality, Love and Eroticism in Modern Societies* (Cambridge, UK: Polity Press, 1992); Zygmunt Bauman, *Liquid Love: On the Frailty of Human Bonds* (Cambridge, UK: Polity Press, 2003).

9. Rhacel Salazar Parreñas, Hung Cam Thai, and Rachel Silvey, "Guest Editors' Introduction—Intimate Industries: Restructuring (Im)Material Labor in Asia," *Positions: Asia Critique* 24, no.1 (2016): 1–15, Project MUSE.

10. Ann L. Stoler, *Carnal Knowledge and Imperial Power: Race and the Intimate Colonial Rule* (Berkeley: University of California Press, 2010); Ann L. Stoler, "Tense and Tender Ties: The Politics of Comparison in North American History and (Post) Colonial Studies," in *Haunted by Empire: Geographies of Intimacy in North American History*, ed. A. L. Stoler (Durham, NC: Duke University Press, 2006), 23–67; Lisa Lowe, *The Intimacies of Four Continents* (Durham, NC: Duke University Press, 2015); Joane Nagel, *Race, Ethnicity, and Sexuality: Intimate Intersections, Forbidden Frontiers* (Oxford: Oxford University Press, 2003).

11. Marcia A. Zug, *Buying a Bride: An Engaging History of Mail-Order Matches* (New York: New York University Press, 2016).

12. Scott Melzer, *Gun Crusaders: The NRA's Culture War* (New York: New York University Press, 2009).

13. Gail Bederman, *Manliness and Civilization: A Cultural History of Gender and Race in the United States, 1880–1917* (Chicago: University of Chicago Press, 2008).

14. Julia Meszaros, "The Manosphere, International Dating and the Crisis of Access," *AG About Gender-International Journal of Gender Studies* 10, no. 19 (2021).

15. Jacqueline Olds and Richard Schwartz, *The Lonely American: Drifting Apart in the Twenty-First Century* (Boston: Beacon Press, 2009).

16. Robert Putnam, *Bowling Alone: The Collapse and Revival of American Community* (New York: Simon & Schuster, 2001).

17. Murthy, Vivek, *Our Epidemic of Loneliness and Isolation: the U.S. Surgeon General's Advisory on the Healing Effects of Social Connection and Community* (Office of the U.S. Surgeon General 2023), https://www.hhs.gov/sites/default/files/surgeon-general-social-connection-advisory.pdf.

18. Eleanor Wilkinson, "The Romantic Imaginary: Compulsory Coupledom and Single Existence," in *Sexualities: Past Reflections, Future Directions* (New York: Springer, 2012), 130–145.

19. Friedrich Engels, *The Origin of the Family, Private Property and the State* (New York: Verso Books, 1972).

20. Giddens, *The Transformation of Intimacy*; Bauman, *Liquid Love*.

21. Arlie Hochschild, *The Second Shift: Working Parents and the Revolution at Home* (New York: Viking Press, 1989).

22. Paula England, "The Gender Revolution: Uneven and Stalled," *Gender & Society* 24, no. 2 (2010):149–166.

23. Lynn Jamieson, "Intimacy Transformed?: A Critical Look at the 'Pure Relationship'," *Sociology* 33, no. 3 (1999): 477–494.

24. Nicole Constable, *Maid to Order in Hong Kong: Stories of Filipina Workers* (Ithaca, NY: Cornell University Press, 1997); Rhacel Parreñas, *Servants of Globalization: Migration and Domestic Work* (Stanford, CA: Stanford University Press, 2015); Lisa Dodson and Rebekah M. Zincavage, "'It's like a Family' Caring Labor, Exploitation, and Race in Nursing Homes," *Gender & Society* 21, no. 6 (2007): 905–928; Arlie Hochschild, "Love and Gold," in *Global Woman: Nannies, Maids and Sex Workers in the New Economy*, ed. B. Ehrenreich and A. Hochschild (New York: Henry Holt, 2002), 15–30.

25. Eileen Boris and Rhacel Salazar Parreñas, eds., *Intimate Labors: Cultures, Technologies, and the Politics of Care* (Stanford, CA: Stanford University Press, 2010), 1–12.

26. Salazar Parreñas et al., "Guest Editors' Introduction—Intimate Industries."

27. Montemurro, *Getting It, Having It, Keeping It Up*.

28. Raewyn Connell, *Masculinities* (Berkeley: University of California Press, 1995).

29. Judith Butler, *Gender Trouble: Feminism and the Subversion of Identity* (New York: Routledge, 2011).

30. Tristan Bridges and C. J. Pascoe, "Hybrid Masculinities: New Directions in the Sociology of Men and Masculinities," *Sociology Compass* 8, no. 3 (2014): 246–258.

31. Rhacel S. Parreñas, *Illicit Flirtations: Labor, Migration, and Sex Trafficking in Tokyo* (Palo Alto, CA: Stanford University Press, 2011); Megan Rivers-Moore, *Gringo Gulch: Sex, Tourism, and Social Mobility in Costa Rica* (Chicago: University of Chicago Press, 2016); Denise Brennan, *What's Love Got to Do With It? Transnational Desires and Sex Tourism in the Dominican Republic* (Durham, NC: Duke University Press, 2004); Amalia Cabezas, *Economies of Desire: Sex and Tourism in Cuba and the Dominican Republic* (Philadelphia: Temple University Press, 2009); Kamala Kempadoo, *Sexing the Caribbean: Gender, Race and Sexual Labor* (New York City: Routledge, 2004); Nicole Constable, *Romance on a*

Global Stage: Pen Pals, Virtual Ethnography, and "Mail Order" Marriages (Berkeley: University of California Press, 2003); Monica Liu, *Seeking Western Men: Email-Order Brides Under China's Global Rise* (Stanford, CA: Stanford University Press, 2022); Felicity Amaya Schaeffer, *Love and Empire: Cybermarriage and Citizenship Across the Americas* (New York: New York University Press, 2013); Anne Allison, *Nightwork: Sexuality, Pleasure and Corporate Masculinity in a Tokyo Hostess Club* (Chicago: University of Chicago Press, 2009); Carolyn Choi, "Moonlighting in the Nightlife: From Indentured to Precarious Labor in Los Angeles Koreatown's Hostess Industry," *Sexualities* 20, no. 4 (2017): 446–462; Parreñas, *Illicit Flirtations.*

32. Ward, *The Tragedy of Heterosexuality*; Rachel O'Neill, *Seduction: Men, Masculinity and Mediated Intimacy* (New York: Wiley, 2018).

33. Yu Kojima, "In the Business of Cultural Reproduction: Theoretical Implications of the Mail-Order Bride Phenomenon," *Women's Studies International Forum* 24, no. 2 (2001): 199–210; Meszaros, "American Men and Romance Tourism."

34. O'Neill, *Seduction.*

35. Cynthia Enloe, *Bananas, Beaches and Bases: Making Feminist Sense of International Politics* (Berkeley: University of California Press, 1990).

36. Ashley Mears, *Very Important People: Status and Beauty in the Global Party Circuit* (Princeton, NJ: Princeton University Press, 2011).

37. Kojima, "In the Business of Cultural Reproduction."

38. Andrew Cherlin, *Labor's Love Lost: The Rise and Fall of the Working-Class Family in America* (New York: Russell Sage Foundation, 2014).

39. O'Neill, *Seduction.*

CHAPTER 3   UKRAINE: THE FRONTIER OF FANTASY

1. Viviana Zelizer, *The Purchase of Intimacy* (Princeton, NJ: Princeton University Press, 2005).

2. Julia Meszaros, "Race, Space, and Agency in the International Introduction Industry: How American Men Perceive Women's Agency in Colombia, Ukraine and the Philippines," *Gender, Place, & Culture* 25, no. 2 (2018): 268–287.

3. Ashley Mears, *Very Important People: Status and Beauty in the Global Party Circuit* (Princeton, NJ: Princeton University Press, 2020).

4. Russian word for grandmother.

5. Harald Fisher-Tine, "'White Women Degrading Themselves to the Lowest Depths': European Networks of Prostitution and Colonial Anxieties in British India and Ceylon ca. 1880–1914," *Indian Economic Social History Review* 40, no. 163 (2003): 163–190; Eileen Scully, "Prostitution as Privilege: The 'American Girl' of Treaty-Port Shanghai, 1860–1937," *The International History Review* 20, no. 4 (1998): 855–883; Philippa Levine, "Orientalist Sociology and the Creation of Colonial Sexualities," *Feminist Review* 65, Summer (2000): 5–17.

6. Masha Gessen, *The Man Without a Face: The Unlikely Rise of Vladimir Putin* (New York: Penguin, 2012).

7. Meszaros, "Race, Space, and Agency."

8. Catherine Hakim, *Erotic Capital: The Power of Attraction in the Boardroom and the Bedroom* (New York: Basic Books, 2011).

9. Tatiana Osipovich, "Russian Mail-Order Brides in U.S. Public Discourse: Sex, Crime, and Cultural Stereotypes," in *Sexuality and Gender in Post Communist Eastern Europe and Russia*, ed. Aleksandar Štulhofer and Theo Sandfort (New York: Routledge, 2005), 231–242.

10. Nicole Constable, *Romance on a Global Stage: Pen Pals, Virtual Ethnography, and "Mail Order" Marriages* (Berkeley: University of California Press, 2003).

11. Ingrid Piller, "Cross-Cultural Communication in Intimate Relationships," in *Handbook of Intercultural Communication*, ed. Helga Kotthoff and Helen Spencer-Oatey, vol. 7 (New York: Mouton de Gruyter, 2007), 341–359.

12. Sonja Luehrmann, "Mediated Marriage: Internet Matchmaking in Provincial Russia," *Europe-Asia Studies* 56, no. 6 (2004): 863.

13. Svitlana Taraban, "Birthday Girls, Russian Dolls and Others: Internet Bride as the Emerging Global Identity of Post-Soviet Women," in *Living Gender After Communism*, ed. Janet Elise Johnson and Jean C. Robinson (Bloomington: Indiana University Press, 2006), 105–127.

14. Brandon Andrew Robinson, "'Personal Preference' as the New Racism: Gay Desire and Racial Cleansing in Cyberspace," *Sociology of Race and Ethnicity* 1, no. 2 (2015): 317–330.

CHAPTER 4   COLOMBIA: THE SEXUALIZED FRONTIER

1. Ann Laura Stoler, *Carnal Knowledge and Imperial Power* (Berkeley: University of California Press, 2002); Evelyn Nakano Glenn, "Racial Ethnic Women's Labor: The Intersection of Race, Gender and Class Oppression," *Review of Radical Political Economics* 17, no. 3 (1985): 86–108; Jennifer Morgan, *Laboring Women: Reproduction and Gender in New World Slavery* (Philadelphia: University of Pennsylvania Press, 2004).

2. Scopolamine is a drug widely used in Colombia by thieves to disorient their victims. People discuss feeling drunk and out of it, being taken to ATMs and told to empty their accounts. The drug is a powder that is usually rubbed into victims' skin.

3. Felicity Amaya Schaeffer, *Love and Empire: Cybermarriage and Citizenship Across the Americas* (New York: New York University Press, 2013).

4. Schaeffer, *Love and Empire*.

5. Schaeffer, *Love and Empire*.

6. María del Mar Sánchez-Fuentes, Sandra Milena Parra-Barrera, and Nieves Moyano, "Cisgender and Transgender Sex Workers from Colombia: The Relation Between Burnout Syndrome and Working Conditions in a Prohibitionist-Regulatory Law," *Sexuality Research and Social Policy* 18 (2021): 507–515; Erin Sanders-McDonagh, *Women and Sex Tourism Landscapes* (New York: Taylor & Francis, 2016); Erica Lorraine Williams, *Sex Tourism in Bahia: Ambiguous Entanglements* (Chicago: University of Illinois Press, 2013); Amalia Cabezas, *Economies of Desire: Sex and Tourism in Cuba and the Dominican Republic* (Philadelphia: Temple University Press, 2009).

7. Denise Brennan, *What's Love Got to Do With It? Transnational Desires and Sex Tourism in the Dominican Republic* (Durham, NC: Duke University Press, 2004).

8. Carol D. Leonnig and David Nakamura, "Secret Service Scandal: Colombian Woman Describes Night of Carousing with Agents," *The Washington Post*, May 4, 2012, https://www.washingtonpost.com/politics/secret-service-scandal-colombian-woman-describes-night-of-carousing-with-agents/2012/05/04/gIQAcwyi1T_story.html.

9. Brennan, *What's Love Got to Do With It?*.

10. Nicole Constable, "Introduction, Cross-Border Marriages, Gendered Mobility and Global Hypergamy," in *Cross Border Marriages: Gender and Mobility in Transnational Asia*, ed. Nicole Constable (Philadelphia: University of Pennsylvania, 2005), 1–16.

11. Ganna Yankovska and Kevin Hannam, "Dark and Toxic Tourism in the Chernobyl Exclusion Zone," *Current Issues in Tourism* 17, no. 10 (2014): 929–939.

12. Hilda Lloréns, "Latina Bodies in the Era of Elective Aesthetic Surgery," *Latino Studies* 11 (2013): 547–569; The term "Maja ideal" comes from the Maja beauty products icon, who is a light-skinned Latina woman with light-colored eyes and long, straight hair.

13. Margaret L. Hunter, *Race, Gender, and the Politics of Skin Tone* (New York: Routledge, 2013), 18.

14. Margarita Chaves and Marta Zambrano, "From Blanqueamiento to Reindigenización: Paradoxes of Mestizaje and Multiculturalism in Contemporary Colombia," *Revista Europea de Estudios Latinoamericanos y del Caribe/European Review of Latin American and Caribbean Studies* (2006): 5–23.

15. Felicity Schaeffer-Grabiel, "Flexible Technologies of Subjectivity and Mobility Across the Americas," *American Quarterly* 58, no. 3 (2006): 891–914.

16. Schaeffer-Grabiel, "Flexible Technologies of Subjectivity."

17. Isabel Molina-Guzmán, *Dangerous Curves: Latina Bodies in the Media*, vol. 5 (New York: New York University Press, 2010).

18. Emily Starr and Michele Adams, "The Domestic Exotic: Mail-Order Brides and the Paradox of Globalized Intimacies," *Signs: Journal of Women in Culture and Society* 41, no. 4 (2016): 953–975.

19. Laura Oso Casas, "Money, Sex, Love and the Family: Economic and Affective Strategies of Latin American Sex Workers in Spain," *Journal of Ethnic and Migration Studies* 36, no. 1 (2010): 47–65; Kamala Kempadoo, *Sexing the Caribbean: Gender, Race, and Sexual Labor* (New York: Psychology Press, 2004).

20. Sara Koopman, "Mona, Mona, Mona! Tropicality and the Imaginative Geographies of Whiteness in Colombia," *Journal of Latin American Geography* 20, no. 1 (2021): 49–78.

21. Starr and Adams, "The Domestic Exotic."

22. Cynthia Enloe, *Bananas, Beaches and Bases: Making Feminist Sense of International Politics* (Berkeley: University of California Press, 1990).

23. Colombian aguardiente is an alcohol made of sugar and anise and is the popular local drink.

CHAPTER 5   PHILIPPINES: THE FRONTIER OF MARRIAGE

1. Nicole Constable, *Romance on a Global Stage: Pen Pals, Virtual Ethnography, and "Mail Order" Marriages* (Berkeley: University of California Press, 2003).

2. Rhacel Salazar Parreñas, "Discipline and Empower: The State Governance of Migrant Domestic Workers," *American Sociological Review* 86, no. 6 (2021): 1043–1065; Robyn Magalit Rodriguez, *Migrants for Export: How the Philippine State Brokers Labor to the World* (Minneapolis: University of Minnesota Press, 2010); Anna Romina Guevarra, *Marketing Dreams, Manufacturing Heroes: The Transnational Labor Brokering of Filipino Workers* (New Brunswick, NJ: Rutgers University Press, 2009).

3. Epifanio San Juan Jr., *U.S. Imperialism and Revolution in the Philippines* (New York: Springer, 2007).

4. Teresita C. del Rosario, "Bridal Diaspora: Migration and Marriage Among Filipino Women," *Indian Journal of Gender Studies* 12, no. 2–3 (2005): 253–273.

5. Andrew Yeo, "Challenging U.S. Military Presence in the Philippines," *South Atlantic Quarterly* 111, no. 4 (2012): 857–864; Victoria Reyes, *Global Borderlands: Fantasy, Violence, and Empire in Subic Bay, Philippines* (Stanford, CA: Stanford University Press, 2020); Vernadette V. Gonzalez, "Military Bases, 'Royalty Trips,' and Imperial Modernities: Gendered and Racialized Labor in the Postcolonial Philippines," *Frontiers: A Journal of Women Studies* 28, no. 3 (2007): 28–59.

6. Gary Hawes, *The Philippine State and the Marcos Regime: The Politics of Export* (Ithaca, NY: Cornell University Press, 2020).

7. The Philippines is the fourth-largest receiving country in terms of remittance incomes, behind India, Mexico, and China. Anri Ichimura, "Despite Pandemic, the Philippines Is Still One of the World's Top Recipients of Remittances Thanks to OFWs," *Esquire*, May 17, 2021, https://www.esquiremag.ph/money/industry/ofw-remittance-4th-world-a00304-20210517.

8. Rhacel Parreñas, *Servants of Globalization: Migration and Domestic Work* (Stanford, CA: Stanford University Press, 2015).

9. According to the Philippine Statistics Authority, in 2021 the majority of OFWs migrated to Asia (78.3 percent), followed by Europe (9.3 percent), then North and South America (8.9 percent), and the main destination is Saudi Arabia (24.4 percent). Philippine Statistics Authority, "Survey on Overseas Filipinos," September 13, 2024, https://psa.gov.ph/statistics/survey/labor-and-employment/survey-overseas-filipinos.

10. Philippine Statistics Authority, "Survey on Overseas Filipinos," September 13, 2024, https://psa.gov.ph/statistics/survey/labor-and-employment/survey-overseas-filipinos.

11. Deirdre McKay, *Filipinas in Canada—De-Skilling as a Push Toward Marriage* (New York: Rowman and Littlefield, 2003); Pei-Chia Lan, "New Global Politics of Reproductive Labor: Gendered Labor and Marriage Migration," *Sociology Compass* 2, no. 6 (2008): 1801–1815; Julia Meszaros, "Marriage Migration as a Pathway to Citizenship: Filipina Brides, Economic Security, and Ideas of Global Hypergamy," in *International Marriages and Marital Citizenship* (New York: Routledge, 2017), 25–40.

12. Lisa Law, "Sex Work in Southeast Asia: The Place of Desire in a Time of AIDS," *Psychology Press* 2 (2000); del Rosario, "Bridal Diaspora."

13. Reyes, *Global Borderlands.*

14. Pia Lee-Brago, "US Envoy Apologizes for Sex Tourism Story," PhilStar Global, October 8, 2011, https://www.philstar.com/headlines/2011/10/08/734751/us-envoy-apologizes-sex-tourism-story.

15. Corrine Redfern, "In Philippine Red-Light District, an Uphill Struggle to Battle Trafficking and Abuses," *The Washington Post*, November 18, 2019, https://www.washingtonpost.com/world/asia-pacific/in-philippine-red-light-district-an-uphill-struggle-to-battle-trafficking-and-abuses/2019/11/17/43a6470a-bad3-11e9-b3b4-2bb69e8c4e39_story.html.

16. Leonora Angeles and Sirijit Sunanta, "'Exotic Love at Your Fingertips': Intermarriage Websites, Gendered Representation, and the Transnational Migration of Filipino and Thai Women," *Kasarinlan: Philippine Journal of Third World Studies* 22, no. 1 (2007): 03–31.

17. Constable, *Romance on a Global Stage*.

18. Constable, *Romance on a Global Stage*, 96.

19. In 1990, the Philippines passed the Anti Mail Order Bride law, which prohibits the business of organizing or facilitating marriages between Filipinas and foreign men. The Republic Act 10906 extended this law into online spaces.

20. Julia Meszaros, "Race, Space, and Agency in the International Introduction Industry: How American Men Perceive Women's Agency in Colombia, Ukraine and the Philippines," *Gender, Place, & Culture* 25, no. 2 (2018): 268–287.

21. U.S. Department of State-Bureau of Consular Affairs, Nonimmigrant Visa Statistics, "Nonimmigrant Visa Issuances by Visa Class and by Nationality," FY2019NIV Detail Table, https://travel.state.gov/content/travel/en/legal/visa-lawo/visa-statistics /nonimmigrant-visa-statistics.html, accessed July 28, 2024. Consistent visa statistics from K-1 visa filings in the past twenty-year period consistently show Filipino migrants accounting for nearly 20 percent of filings.

22. Cecilia Tacoli, "International Migration and the Restructuring of Gender Asymmetries: Continuity and Change Among Filipino Labor Migrants in Rome," *International Migration Review* 33, no. 3 (1999): 658–682.

23. U.S. Department of State, "Philippines Travel Advisory: Philippines-Level 2: Exercise Increased Caution," https://travel.state.gov/content/travel/en/traveladvisories/travel advisories/philippines-travel-advisory.html, accessed July 28, 2024.

24. Sisig is a dish made from pig's face and belly with onions and chili peppers.

25. Constable, *Romance on a Global Stage*.

CHAPTER 6   MARRIAGE: HAPPILY EVER AFTER?

1. Stephanie Coontz, *Marriage, a History: How Love Conquered Marriage* (New York: Penguin, 2006); Arlie Hochschild and Anne Machung, *The Second Shift: Working Families and the Revolution at Home* (New York: Penguin, 2012); Paula England, "The Gender Revolution: Uneven and Stalled," *Gender & Society* 24, no. 2 (2010):149–166.

2. Matthew Hayes, "'We Gained a Lot Over What We Would Have Had': The Geographic Arbitrage of North American Lifestyle Migrants to Cuenca, Ecuador," *Journal of Ethnic and Migration Studies* 40, no. 12 (2014): 1953–1971.

3. Hochschild and Machung, *The Second Shift*.

4. Julia Meszaros, "American Men and Romance Tourism: Searching for Traditional Trophy Wives as Status Symbols of Masculinity," *WSQ: Women's Studies Quarterly* 45, no. 1 (2017): 225–242.

5. Kate Manne, *Down Girl: The Logic of Misogyny* (New York: Oxford University Press, 2017).

6. Anthony Giddens, *The Transformation of Intimacy: Sexuality, Love and Eroticism in Modern Societies* (Oxford, UK: Polity Press, 1992).

7. Jane Ward, *The Tragedy of Heterosexuality* (New York: New York University Press, 2022).

8. Christian Rudder, *Dataclysm: Love, Sex, Race, and Identity—What Our Online Lives Tell Us About Our Offline Selves* (New York: Broadway Books, 2014).

9. Wanjohi Kibicho, *Sex Tourism in Africa: Kenya's Booming Industry* (New York: Routledge, 2016).

10. A sari-sari store is typically a small local sundry store that is operated independently. These stores sell snacks, drinks, and sundries like dish and laundry soap in small quantities.

11. Mike Hawkins, "Liberty Call at Sunset: U.S. Military Retiree Bars and the Outsourced Reproduction of Ageing Masculinities in Subic Bay, Philippines," *Cultural Geographies* 29, no. 2 (2022): 219–232.

INDEX

"act of love," reproductive labor as, 92

Adams, John: age gap recommendation of, 132; appeal of Colombian women explained by, 94; author's fieldwork and, 14–16; early Russian and Ukraine operations of, 24–25, 71; popularity of Ukrainian women explained by, 79–81, 86; safety and vetting services of, 25

Adams, Michele, 96

aesthetic labor, 4–12; activities included in, 8; of Colombian women, 18, 53–54, 61–63, 88, 91–94, 104, 126; as component of emotional labor, 8; denied, misogyny as repercussion for, 11–12; femininity capital from, 6–10, 11; of Filipino women, 63, 105–106, 123–124, 126; industry's reliance on, 20–21, 46–47, 60; intimate frontiers for extracting, 14; male hierarchy based on access to, 5, 13–14, 17, 20–21; market logics and, 60–66; masculinity based on extraction of, 126–127; men's expectations for, 4–5, 12, 53–54; perceived decline in West, 46; race and, 10–11; reproductive labor less valued than, 5, 62; of Russian women, 24, 53–54; stereotypical beauty standards and, 11; of trans women, 9–10; of Ukrainian women, 18, 34, 41–42, 54, 65, 68, 71, 81–82, 86, 126

aesthetic nationalism, in Colombia, 91, 96

AFA. See A Foreign Affair

affiliate marketers, 29–30

A Foreign Affair (AFA): author's fieldwork involving, 14–16; Colombian labor extracted by, 100–104; COVID-19 pandemic and, 133; early Russian and Ukraine operations of, 24–25, 71; establishment of, 24; as first internet-only agency, 24; introductory seminars of, 70–71; local partners of, 35–36; racialized hierarchy of tours, 11; romance tours in Philippines, 106; romance tours in Ukraine, 68, 70–75; safety and vetting offered by, 25; scam prevention efforts of, 132; Ukrainian labor extracted by, 82–86; Ukrainian operations suspended by, 133

Africa, racialized hierarchy and, 11, 127

AfricaBeauties, 24

age: and "baggage" of older women in U.S., 114; of desirable women (younger/age gap), 19, 26–27, 30, 64, 111–118, 123–124, 127, 132; and desire for children, 52, 112, 115, 132; of Filipino women, 19, 64, 111–118, 123–124, 132; of male participants, 26; of marriageable women in Ukraine, 36; and "zones of success," 33

agency business model, 27–29

American Asian Worldwide Services, 24

American Sociological Association, 2

AmoLatina, 24

AnastasiaDate, 24, 27–29, 133

Anastasia International, 24

Angeles City, Philippines, 107–108

Anti Mail Order Bride law (Philippines), 149n19

arbitrage, geographic, 13, 125, 132

artificial intelligence (AI), 29

AsianBeauties, 24

Asian women, as war brides, 22–23

Australia: Filipino labor and migration in, 18–19, 107; men from, dating in Philippines, 16, 112, 118, 121, 130; men from, frustration with feminism, 34; visa requirements of, 112

Badu (website), 43

Baltimore, Maryland, author's fieldwork in, 15

Barranquilla, Colombia, 18, 96–97

beauty standards, stereotypical, 11, 127

"beauty work," 8. See also aesthetic labor

Bederman, Gail, 50

Belarus, author's fieldwork in, 15, 36

Besuden, David, 24

Besuden, Elena, 24

Black men, as participants in international dating, 2, 15

Black women: reproductive labor of, 7–8, 10–11; stereotypical beauty standards and, 11, 127

blanqueamiento (whitening), 96

blogging, 31

Boris, Eileen, 8–9

boutique matchmaking: in Colombia, 42–46; local, 33, 35–46; in Philippines, 108; sociological principles used in, 37–38; in Ukraine, 33, 35–42, 68, 73, 87, 133–134; women's labor in, 21

ABOUT THE AUTHOR

JULIA H. MESZAROS is an associate professor at East Texas A&M University. Her work on the "mail order bride" industry appears in a number of scholarly sources, such as *Women's Studies Quarterly* and *Men and Masculinities.* During her free time, she enjoys pickleball, yoga, and spending time with her cats.

Available titles in The Politics of Marriage and Gender: Global Issues in Local Contexts series:

Xiaoling Shu and Jingjing Chen, *Chinese Marriages in Transition: From Patriarchy to New Familism*

Helena Zeweri, *Between Care and Criminality: Marriage, Citizenship, and Family in Australian Social Welfare*

Julia H. Meszaros, *Economies of Gender: Masculinity, "Mail Order Brides," and Women's Labor*